# A Field Guide to Good Decisions

# A Field Guide to Good Decisions

## Values in Action

Mark D. Bennett and
Joan McIver Gibson

Westport, Connecticut
London

**Library of Congress Cataloging-in-Publication Data**

Bennett, Mark D.
    A field guide to good decisions: values in action / Mark D. Bennett
and Joan McIver Gibson.
        p. cm.
    Includes bibliographical references and index.
    ISBN 0–275–98937–2 (alk. paper)
    1. Decision making.    I. Gibson, Joan McIver.    II. Title.
HD30.23.B462    2006
153.8'3—dc22          2005034800

British Library Cataloguing in Publication Data is available.

Library of Congress Catalog Card Number: 2005034800
ISBN: 0–275–98937–2

First published in 2006

Praeger Publishers, 88 Post Road West, Westport, CT 06881
An imprint of Greenwood Publishing Group, Inc.
www.praeger.com

Printed in the United States of America

∞

The paper used in this book complies with the
Permanent Paper Standard issued by the National
Information Standards Organization (Z39.48–1984).

10   9   8   7   6   5   4   3   2   1

For Nancy Hoffman and Stephen King,
friends, allies, and champions

# Contents

# Acknowledgments

We are grateful to all the advocates for decision-making integrity who believed in us and welcomed us into their organizations: Wendell Jones, Jack Dickey, Nancy Hoffman, Stephen King, Don Noack, Gail Szenasi, Valerie Ford, Judy Jones, Sig Olson, Catherine McClain, Leslie Cryer, Mette Pedersen, Paul Roth, Julie Rosen, Tres Schnell and Jennifer Metzler.

We salute the leaders and managers of Centura Health who attended our seminars over the past eight years. They live this book every day. Their work with us as students, colleagues, and facilitators gave us fertile ground in which to grow our ideas and tools to hone our approach. Special thanks go to Sharon Tuelp, Con Kelly, Lou Krippel, and Ginger Morgan.

We thank our special friends and colleagues who understand how to bridge culture differences with respect, shared stories, and wisdom from the front lines: Lucy Moore, Rosemary Romero, Gayle Dine Chacon, Teresa Burke, Anne Simpson, Hajra Malik, and Vardit Ravitsky.

As all writers learn, the support and sacrifices of family are remarkable. To Mickey Gibson, Dottie Smith, Sheila Conneen, David Johnson, and Andrew, Chris, and Dorothy Bennett, our abundant thanks can never be sufficient, but they are indeed necessary.

Our team of skilled coaches—advocates for writing clarity and reader sensitivity—did not spare our feelings and encouraged us to "say it directly and with fewer words": April Kopp, Julie Reichert, Kay Hagan, Corin Wood, and Barbara Bennett Rivera.

Thank you, Hilary Claggett of Praeger, who first encouraged us. And thank you, Nick Philipson, our senior editor and indefatigable guide.

Finally, each of us has particular allies who strengthened and encouraged us at important moments during this journey.

Joan: Rob Schwartz, David Bennahum, and Stewart Duban invited me into their professional homes and made me feel welcome. The GYRLZ, Steve Miles, Nancy Dubler, and Ruth Purtilo continue to shine brighter than most. Neil and Judith Morgan counseled patience and a rereading of Strunk and White's *Elements of Style*. Robin Gibson keeps me honest and makes me laugh. Mike Gibson keeps me sane and in love. The late Miriam McIver is my light.

Mark: First, last, and always, my wife and best friend, Nancy Woodward: her presence nourishes my spirit and encourages me on my path. Tom Daly stepped into my life at a critical moment with the gifts of insight and awareness. Jeff Hood blessed me with deep listening and good questions. Victor LaCerva modeled perseverance and a "can-do" spirit. Marilyn Mason encouraged me as only a true elder can. Merle Lefkoff, Deborah Boldt, and Bill Conway offered encouragement and contacts.

# Preface

For over a decade before we met, each of us worked with people facing difficult choices. Joan was the chair of a hospital ethics committee, and Mark was a professional mediator of business, family, and community disputes. We participated in many decisions at conference tables and hospital bedsides. We supported people as they made choices that shaped their professional and personal lives. We watched and we learned.

The road to this book began in 1990, when Joan attended one of Mark's mediation trainings, looking for ways to improve bioethics consultations. Our first project as colleagues explored the use of mediation to assist families and medical professionals struggling with end-of-life decisions. We moved on to consult with organizations on ways to build a culture of accountability and transparency in decision-making.

In our work with organizations, from small, mission-driven nonprofit organizations to large, complex corporations, we have observed two recurring patterns. First, people are uncomfortable with direct exchanges about values, principles, and ethics. Second, failure to conduct healthy conversations about what really matters lowers the bar for ethical decision-making, especially when there is pressure to make difficult decisions quickly.

The result is a minimalist approach to ethics and decision-making. Anything that does not directly violate law or policy becomes ethical and acceptable. Because departments pass ethics audits by virtue of having broken no laws or rules, ethics has become synonymous with compliance.

We believe that compliance with law and policy is necessary but not sufficient for an ethical and effective decision. Ethics is not simply about turning away from what is wrong or bad, but about turning toward what is right and good. We make good decisions, decisions that work, when we understand and act on what we believe is important, when we anticipate the consequences of our decisions on others, and when we hold ourselves accountable for our decisions.

This book weaves together threads from our separate and joint work with individuals, families, groups, and organizations. Our experiences on the ground, for over twenty-five years, provide the perspective and inspiration to map the road to a good decision.

Wendell Jones, a wise colleague and veteran observer of decisions in a large, complex organization, offered us a powerful metaphor when he observed that senior managers and leaders in organizational life do not produce services or goods. They produce decisions. If decisions are products, then we have been involved in the repair business for many years. We usually intervene when decisions have begun to break down. After many years of repair work, we have concluded that a clear process, careful attention to values, and some degree of reflection are necessary to "manufacture" good decisions. We wrote this field guide to help people make good decisions that should not need repair.

Many books about decision-making describe the climate in major corporation boardrooms or the halls of power in Washington, DC. Most of us do not breathe this air. For every large corporation, CEO, and governor, there are thousands of small and medium-sized businesses, managers, agency supervisors, mayors, and city councilors. In every community citizens serve on the governing boards of churches, nonprofit organizations, public and private schools, and neighborhood associations. They make the tough choices necessary to further their organizations' missions. Their business is nothing less than the health, vitality, and livability of our communities.

Families are not exempt from making difficult decisions. They face wrenching choices about finances, job security, health care insurance, assisted living for elderly parents, and end-of-life care for themselves and loved ones. When family members gather around a kitchen table to grapple with issues of life, quality of life, and death, they must be able to talk with depth and respect about what matters.

Many books about decision-making emphasize theory, philosophy, and abstract moral principles while shortchanging immediate, practical assistance. This book fills that gap in three ways:

- We focus on **transferable skills** for making good decisions in the workplace, community, and home.
- We show how to **talk productively about values** without defensiveness, arrogance, or value-to-value combat.
- We describe a fresh approach to **bridging cultural differences**.

When a difficult choice presents itself, people need traction. Traction on the road to a good decision comes from deliberate, honest, and respectful talk about what matters. We wrote this book to bring the language of values and ethics alive at every conference and kitchen table. Tough choices and good decisions demand nothing less.

# Introduction: The Territory

*One's philosophy is not best expressed in words; it is expressed in the choices one makes. In the long run, we shape our lives and we shape ourselves. The process never ends until we die. And the choices we make are ultimately our responsibility.*

**Eleanor Roosevelt**

Like it or not, life is about choices. Many of these choices require nothing more than personal reflection or a snap judgment: which movie to see, the brand of car to buy, or even an important decision like whether to embark on an expensive home-remodeling project. This book does not concern itself with these types of choices. Our focus is on difficult choices that affect others. Such choices are difficult because you cannot possibly honor every value or please everyone. You have to compromise important interests. Others may suffer. Yet you must choose. How do you face these challenges and create a good decision?

Making a good decision requires that you engage others, know your own role, and accept responsibility for your choice, warts and all.

Good decisions require that you engage others in reflecting on what matters to each of you. Beyond talk, of course, is the courage to act on your values. This book describes the road from values to action and how to bring integrity into decisions you make in your work and professional life, your family, your neighborhood, and your community.

Every difficult choice is like a dramatic play in which you have one of three parts. You may be the decision-maker, acting individually or as a member of a group. You may be a member of the supporting cast, providing input or exerting influence as you advise and consult with the decision-maker. You may be an interested party, someone who is not involved in making the decision but will be affected by the outcome.

Your part—the lines you speak, the emotion of your delivery, the intensity of your participation—flows from your real-life roles. In a family decision about job relocation, you may be a parent, spouse, and midcareer professional. In a civic issue about environmental pollution in your town, you may be a parent, concerned citizen, and advocate. In an organizational controversy about layoffs, you may be a board member, colleague, and friend. No matter what the situation, each of us usually plays more than one role.

This is a book about practical ethics. Our most challenging choices are not about good vs. bad or right vs. wrong. Rather, they are choices between competing goods, daily decisions we encounter in our families, communities, nonprofit organizations, and businesses. Consider a few examples. A family struggles to keep aging parents safe while honoring their desire to remain independent. A community weighs homeowners' concerns about safety and property values against the need to provide shelter for the homeless. A business must consider the costs and benefits of laying off loyal employees to remain financially viable. A nonprofit board and staff must determine the best use of inadequate resources to address important social needs.

While these decisions are dissimilar and bear little or no resemblance to each other, there is one common thread. The decision-makers need to make good decisions in difficult situations, where some values advance and others yield.

> *The map is not the territory.*
> **Alfred Korzybski**

These decisions have both benefits and downsides. The decision-makers bear responsibility for the total package.

## BUILDING A ROAD

What is a good decision? A good decision resolves an issue or responds effectively to an event. A good decision considers those who must implement it. A good decision anticipates negative consequences and aims for a preponderance of benefits. A good decision does not require that everyone be happy with the result or agree with the decision-maker. A good decision reflects the integrity of the decision-making process. In short, good decisions work.

Integrity is a big word. Commentators routinely bemoan the absence of integrity, whether in the form of CEOs' and political leaders' shortcomings, celebrities' moral lapses, or the media's repeated violations of public sensibilities. Few who use the term "integrity" define what they mean. Most speak only about the space left when integrity is missing in action.

Some authors define integrity as a dimension of a decision-maker's character. Others define it as a stand-alone quality of a decision or action, without regard to process or context. Our emphasis is different. For us, a decision-maker builds integrity as she goes. Complete decisions, decisions made with integrity, feature three elements: they are whole, coherent, and transparent. The process of reaching such a decision is deliberate and always makes space for reflection. Even when decisions must be made quickly, reflection is always possible, always important. Without it, any decision is incomplete and more likely to fail.

First, decisions made with integrity are whole. A building has structural integrity when all necessary supporting components are present, solid, and connected, from the foundation to the roof. An important decision requires similar attention if it is to stand and endure. The foundation stones for all significant decisions are our values. We choose and decide based on what is important to us. A decision is whole and sound when we've done the homework and understand what is involved. We've talked with, or at least thought about, others who deserve to be considered. Finally, before we act, we have reflected on what really matters. We have covered the bases.

Second, decisions made with integrity are coherent. Coherence comes when the reasons we give for our decision actually align with the decision itself. Coherence is not accidental. We create it. When we deliberately integrate our beliefs and actions, we walk our talk. There is more to good decision-making than facing difficult situations with courage, acting with resolve, and believing that doing so is sufficient. Missing is the up-front work of considering important values, others' and ours. When our reasons and values resonate with our decisions, coherence is obvious. Good decisions are coherent.

Finally, good decisions are transparent. Without direct, on-the-level communication, integrity suffers. Every week, newspapers feature exposés of political corruption, government cover-ups, or business scandals. Op-ed columnists lament the absence of accountability in public and political arenas. Nationwide, our citizens report that they just don't believe what they read and hear. Accountability and trust rest on openness and honesty. When we speak directly and candidly to others about our decision and its impact, we become accountable for our choice. Integrity requires telling the truth, including the hard parts.

It is difficult to achieve integrity in decision-making by ourselves. Reflection and careful consideration benefit from different perspectives. Our challenging, important choices become more solid and complete when we engage others. Even when we can, or must, make a decision alone, our action reaches beyond us. It may affect family members, fellow employees, or others. We may need to listen to individuals or groups who, though not directly affected, have important concerns. Consulting others can strengthen the decision and increase the chances of successful implementation.

The following five steps move us along the road to a good decision:

1. **Clarify** the perspective others and we bring to the issue.
2. **Comprehend** the range of what matters to others and us.
3. **Commit** to what is most important that will guide the decision.
4. **Choose** a course of action that aligns with the most important values.
5. **Communicate** the decision to others openly and honestly.

A good decision, one that is whole, coherent, and transparent, succeeds at each step. A decision's integrity mirrors the quality of the decision-maker's process. While character and intent matter, as does the ethical content of the final decision, no book can dictate to you what a good decision is in your particular situation. This book shows you how to build your own road and travel it to a good decision.

> *Nothing in life is to be feared.*
> *It is only to be understood.*
> **Madame Curie**

## TALKING VALUES

Many people become nervous at the prospect of talking openly about values. Some are anxious about unleashing passions and encountering strongly held, irreconcilable views. Others fear a kind of conversational black hole that devours precious time and energy without producing concrete results.

We use the term "values" broadly to mean whatever matters to you, to your organization, and to your community. Values include meaningful obligations to others, such as honesty, fairness, respect, and compassion. There are values necessary for smooth functioning, such as efficiency, usefulness, accessibility, physical security, and tradition. Values also include what we desire: friendship, economic security, success, simplicity, and inner peace. Values are present in every domain of life, from personal to professional, economic to aesthetic, and political to spiritual.

Values are the foundations of our opinions, preferences, choices, and decisions. We cannot and do not make value-free decisions. When a choice is difficult, we need clarity about what matters, to us and to others. Values talk as commonly practiced doesn't seem to help. It tends to be pretentious. It often enlists heavy, emotion-charged words that, while powerfully stated, are poorly defined. This kind of talk gets in the way of good decision-making. Avoiding values, however, does not banish them. They remain powerful and present, even though veiled from our understanding.

Advocating more talk about values is not without risk. After the 2004 U.S. presidential election, journalists and pundits speculated on the influence of moral values concerns on the outcome, a reminder that the topic of values in public and private conversation is neither neutral nor universally affirming. Political groups, religious activists, and social commentators of all stripes use terms like moral values, family values, religious values, and American values to elevate their own cause or attack opponents. Much of the current public discourse about values divides and polarizes.

No group owns the topic of values or the territory of values conversation. We want people across the political, religious, and cultural spectrum to reclaim the word "values." Strong, useful values conversation is a second language that everyone needs to speak in common spaces. For a family, this space may be a meeting around the kitchen table. For a business, it may be a strategy meeting of a senior management team in the CEO's office. For a community, it may be a school board or city council study session.

Traction on the road to a good decision requires solid footing. Reassuring contact comes when we illuminate important values, both ours and those of others. Good decisions depend on engaging others at this level of meaning and importance. We need to overcome our anxiety and resistance to values talk, especially when the going is tough and the choices are hard.

We describe a step-by-step process for talking about difficult issues where important values bump up against each other. The goal is illumination instead of irritation and respect in place of recrimination. We want you to engage with values, not as weapons or tools of debate but as demanding, guiding stars that help you, in the company of others, navigate the road to a good decision.

Our approach is simple in concept, but it is not easy to practice. It demands careful listening instead of waiting to interrupt. It insists on making abstract values language concrete and clear. We will show you how to replace jargon and inflammatory rhetoric with ordinary, direct language. Values talk becomes productive and meaningful when you and others give voice to what matters and why. Values come alive when you bring abstract concepts down to earth, plant them in a specific setting, and grow an understanding of their meaning.

When the time for talk is over and you must choose, we will give you specific ways to use the most important values to point the way. If you have become confident and clear about what matters and you have the courage to act on what matters most, you honor Eleanor Roosevelt's admonition to shape your life and live your personal philosophy.

## BRIDGING DIFFERENCES

As a decision-maker, you come with your own history and way of seeing an issue. No matter what hat you wear (that of CEO, spouse, teacher, executive, etc.), you bring past experience, role expectations, and ingrained habits of problem solving. However, dilemmas arise at specific times, in specific places, and involve or affect specific people. To make a good decision, you need to understand and work within its unique context. The road to a good decision runs through territory inhabited by others. When crucial values are in tension or conflict, individuals and groups will care deeply about what is at stake or at risk. Difficult choices arouse intensity and passion.

> It is easier to build walls than it is to build bridges.
> **Isaac Newton**

We all have histories and different ways of seeing and understanding the world. Add intensity and passion to these differences and you get a volatile mixture that may resemble TV wrestling or a verbal food fight more than a respectful, enlightening conversation.

One way to get your arms around the challenge of people and their differences is to expand your view of culture. Go beyond the usual understanding that stops at such observable characteristics as race, ethnicity, and national origin. Culture is more than black and white, Latino and Anglo, Arab and Jew, Christian and Muslim, or French and English. Culture embraces a complex set of elements that shape the way each of us sees and makes sense of the world. These elements include education, language, identity, social structure, belief system, and socioeconomic background.

For example, substantial differences in worldviews come from our education and training. A colleague in health care summarizes this well. "*Doctor speaks doctor, nurse speaks nurse, and nobody speaks patient.*" Moreover, within every identifiable culture there are differences. Within doctor culture, pediatricians and orthopedic surgeons see the world and resolve problems differently, based on their different disciplines and training.

Different identities such as gender influence how we see and speak about the world. The linguist Deborah Tannen points out that gender-related social influences and behavior norms produce remarkable differences in how women and men talk and understand what's being said. Most of us know this from direct, sometimes painful, experience.

Consider belief systems. Although both a conservative Baptist and a liberal Episcopalian may be white, middle class, and well educated, they may speak a different language when talking about matters of faith, scripture, and social policy. Owners of small farms and urban environmental activists may not know how to begin a conversation about effective planning for the health of a watershed.

Cultural differences are everywhere and challenge our ability to talk together, understand each other, and learn from others. Without intention and attention, differences can overwhelm. Passion-fueled differences polarize. As you build the road to a good decision and attempt to bring values alive in conversation, you will need to bridge cultural divides. A way to begin is by taking stock of your own set of diverse cultural influences. You are, after all, a multicultural phenomenon in your own right.

To build a bridge of respect, begin with a simple yet powerful acknowledgement that differences exist and are acceptable. Then try something harder: consider the possibility that someone with a different way of seeing and understanding may have knowledge or insight that you don't have, yet may need. Be open, curious, and willing to learn.

Whether the issue is personal, professional, or intergovernmental, you can choose to value differences instead of fearing them. Learning from others who see differently helps pave the road to a good decision.

## STRUCTURE

We have divided this book into two parts. Part I provides a road-building map in the form of a five-step process. We organize each step around a fundamental challenge or question you must address on the road to a good decision. The cumulative product is a decision made and communicated with integrity. For a snapshot of the five steps, see "Summary of the Steps" in the Appendix.

Part II looks more carefully at difficult terrain where you may lose your way. We examine predictable obstacles in thinking, culture, and organizational life. For each obstacle, we guide you in skillful navigation and staying on track.

Throughout this book, "we" includes all of us together, on the road, as we explore the territory. We have guided others through this territory for years. Yet, like you, we continue to make our own journeys, facing difficult choices as parents, spouses, professionals, and citizens. We must address the same challenges, as do you and the people described in this book. We are not experts apart from you but seasoned travelers who continue to walk similar roads. Therefore, we choose to place ourselves beside you as we share what we have observed and learned.

Important decisions are milestones in our lives. As Robert Frost says in "The Road Not Taken," our choices "make all the difference." There is a road leading to every important decision. The journey along that road tells a story. Therefore, we begin each chapter with a story of family, work, or community. Our stories are composites of people we know and situations we've encountered, recreated in a fresh form that preserves confidences while remaining real.

# Part I

## The Road to a Good Decision

# 1

## Clarify Perspective

*We see the world, not the way it is, but the way we are.*

**Talmud**

Imagine a courtyard surrounded on all sides by a multistory building. Each building side facing the courtyard is arrayed with windows, and each window offers a unique view of the courtyard. Windows on the ground floor reveal a different aspect than those in the penthouse. Some window frames are large, permitting a broad area to be observed. Others are small, even tiny. The window glass may be clear or partially opaque, filtering and limiting the view.

The courtyard symbolizes any situation where we face a difficult decision; the windows represent varying perspectives and points of view. No matter the nature of the decision, each of us stands somewhere in that building— that is, somewhere in relation to the issues, the people, and other important elements of the situation. From where we stand, each of us sees, or fails to see, certain dimensions of the situation, available choices, and the solution that fits best with what matters to us. When we address the situation, we can only speak from our unique perspective. When we listen to others, our perspective colors what we hear.

In making decisions, our first challenge is to assess where we stand and how we look at the issues. Our vantage point and angle of view may leave blind spots. Parts of the situation (people, values, information) may be difficult or impossible to see. If we jump in and rush to judgment, we increase the likelihood that we will fail to consider important elements. We increase the risk of making flawed decisions.

While perspective may impede a thoughtful, wise decision, it can also illuminate. We need perspective to analyze any situation and try to make sense of what is involved. Perspective shapes the process of thinking about what to do and how to choose the path forward. Throughout the book we use the word "frame" to denote a specific kind of perspective that controls what is important or less important in the decision-making process.

> As a rule we perceive what we expect to perceive.... The unexpected is usually not received at all. It is not seen or heard, but ignored. Or it is misunderstood.
>
> **Peter Drucker**

This chapter shows how to understand the **elements that shape our own perspective**; work with **frames** and benefit from other points of view; and **change frames** to improve personal perspective.

## A FAMILY AT THE CROSSROADS

Ruth and John Bates and their daughter Sally are seated around the dinner table. Sally is seventeen and suffers from relatively mild cerebral palsy. Ruth is excited. She puts down her fork and makes an announcement:

> "Guess what guys? Don Simpson called me today. John, remember Don? He was my boss's boss when I started here at Temple College, and we always really got along. Well, now he happens to be president of Preston University in Ohio. He called to tell me the provost position is open there, and he more than hinted that I'd be a strong candidate for the position, if I applied. Can you believe it? Talk about my dream job! Not only that, but I'd double my salary. We'd have a housing allowance, unbelievable benefits, and a generous pension. And Sally—there'd be free tuition for family members. With your grades and SAT scores, I'm sure you'd be admitted. What do you two think?"

So what's the decision here? A woman has the opportunity to land her dream job at twice her current pay and with fabulous benefits. Where's the dilemma?

Then John weighs in. His first inclination is to be proud and supportive of Ruth. But he's looking through a different window, and his view is somewhat different.

> "Hey, that's great Ruth. You should be really flattered. But whoa—let me get my breath. Sure, I guess I could start up another landscaping business in Ohio. All I have to do is learn what kinds of trees grow there—ha ha that's a joke. Maybe with you bringing in the big bucks it wouldn't be so important anyway. And it sure would be great to start piling up a nest egg for Sally's future. What do you think, kiddo?"

Sally's window is pretty narrow, and right now she's seeing only one thing—disaster.

"Thanks a lot, mom! How could you even think of dragging me away from here my senior year in high school? I've worked like a dog to get where I am—to finally have really good friends who've supported me and given me the confidence to run for class president next year. And I won! I can't believe you want me to start all over someplace I've never even heard of. Besides, you know Amy and Joyce and I have a plan to all go to the same college."

Now we have a more comprehensive view of the courtyard. The dream job involves a distant move, which would remove Sally from her hard-won support network. Ruth is motivated—at least partly—by her hopes and concerns for her daughter. The reality of Sally's future medical bills has weighed on both parents for years. John is a talented landscape architect, but his work is irregular and often seasonal. This job offers Ruth the means to provide for the economic security of her family. John knows that if his work is spotty here, it will be even more so in a place where he knows no one. Sally knows better than anyone else does how hard it would be to make new friends her senior year in a strange place. None of the three has explicitly mentioned Sally's condition, even though it's paramount in each of their minds. So far, it remains the elephant in the courtyard.

## ELEMENTS THAT SHAPE PERSPECTIVE

Like the components of a metal alloy, three powerful elements forge our individual perspectives: roles we play, life experience, and training.

### Roles

Everyone inhabits multiple roles in life: parent, spouse, partner, friend, neighbor, citizen, mentor, supervisor, coworker, son, or daughter. Think of roles as hats. Each hat brings with it responsibilities, expectations, and values. Some situations require that we wear more than one hat, balancing the responsibilities each places on us. Then there are times when a situation propels one of our roles into the lead. Ruth is wearing at least three hats as she considers this unexpected job opportunity: wife, mother, and professional academic. As she weighs her options and considers the best course of action, one of these roles, with its values, may take precedence.

Multiple roles produce conflicting values. We've touched on Ruth's role as wife and mother. As an academic administrator, she is at the height of her professional powers and has personal goals for advancement and challenge.

Later that evening, John reminds Ruth that she is wearing yet another hat. "Ruthie, have you thought about what this move would mean for your folks?

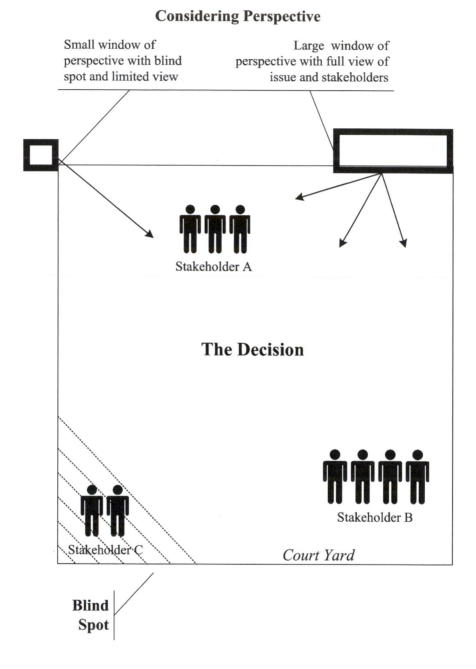

# Considering Perspective

Small window of perspective with blind spot and limited view

Large window of perspective with full view of issue and stakeholders

Stakeholder A

**The Decision**

Stakeholder B

Stakeholder C

*Court Yard*

**Blind Spot**

If we move to Ohio, we'll be 800 miles away from them. And without us here to help, they can't stay in their home. They'll have to move into assisted living, and we both know how strongly they feel about that."

Ruth's first response is a quick retort: "John, please don't bring my parents into this. My sisters moved away and I stayed here. I've always been the one taking care of them—and so far that's been fine. I love them and I've been happy to help. But I won't make this decision based only on what they need. I want to do what's best for you, me, and Sally. I'm sorry, but that's how I feel."

For Ruth, the importance she places on providing for Sally's security after she and John are unable to watch over her clearly flows from her maternal role. The job's promise to accomplish this may loom large, making it difficult to consider other important viewpoints. Ruth also sees her daughter, as a young woman, beginning to make her own plans and wanting to assert her independence. This important

> *Everyone is a prisoner of his own experiences. No one can eliminate prejudices, just recognize them.*
> **Edward R. Murrow**

transition is one that most parents want to facilitate. Within a role there can be tension between goals, in this case between Sally's security and her freedom.

### Life Experience

Experience with people and issues also colors our perspective. These interactions shape our current outlook. Relationships are connections between people, defined by shared experiences. Relationships are different from roles. For example, the role of a brother to three sisters may prompt in him a sense of obligation to respect and love each of them. But in truth, his history with each and his feelings of affinity and trust for each are completely different. These differences cause him to spend time and communicate with them in unique ways. Prior experience with someone may also generate trust or mistrust. We may have been through difficult times together and earned trust the hard way. We may have known each other for years or only recently met. Perhaps we worked together in the distant past but don't know each other well, and so on.

As humans, we bring our own historic baggage into and out of relationships and situations. Each of us, facing a difficult decision, may have an item or two that we don't want to discuss but that will color what we are thinking. For example, while Ruth is sympathetic to her husband and daughter's reservations about moving, she also realizes that at fifty-five she will never get a chance like this again. Her present job has grown tiresome and repetitive, and this is an opportunity to be excited about work again, to make a difference. She harbors some resentment because, while her sisters moved away to follow their husbands and careers, she stayed and became their parents' prime caregiver. It's about time they took a turn.

As for John, he's nearly sixty, and his life is pretty comfortable the way it is. He'd never admit it, but maybe he's just a tiny bit jealous of Ruth's flashy new job and all the attention she may be getting. And how will he ever replace Ed, Toby, and the rest of the Saturday morning golf crew?

Sally may be just plain afraid. Afraid she doesn't have it in her to begin again. Maybe she won't like her new doctors. Who will her friends be?

All these relationships and experiences not only influence how and what we see, but they also affect how we communicate. Along with this personal history come assumptions and judgments that determine our perspective. Relationships vary in strength and intensity. As we saw, Ruth has a significant level of resentment toward her sisters and their lack of responsibility in caring for their parents. These feelings may interfere with her willingness or ability to look at how her decision will affect them. She may not be able to hear and consider their concerns.

Ruth's decision will affect many people with whom she has relationships: John, Sally, Ruth's parents, Ruth's sisters, Sally's friends, Ruth and John's friends, Ruth's coworkers, John's clients, and others. All of these people are stakeholders. Their stakes in the decision may be direct and substantial or indirect and small. Individuals, groups, and organizations array themselves around a decision. Each of them also brings a point of view. Whether or not they participate in the discussion, they may need to support or bless the decision in some way. Without their approval or acceptance, the decision might not be supportable.

Powerful experiences outside of personal relationships come into play and affect perspective as well. What if Ruth has turned down several attractive offers over the years and sees this as the last chance to fulfill her deferred professional dreams? Perhaps her parents taught her that higher education and professional advancement are the benchmarks of a successful life.

As we grow up, we receive both explicit and tacit instructions about feeling, thinking, and relating. These instructions come from our families, the groups we belong to, and the communities where we live and work. Core teachings from our cultural upbringing embed deeply in our psyche. They shape what and how we see. For example, parents, relatives, and community members may telegraph to the younger generation the importance of working hard and fully employing one's talents and skills. Through words and examples, a young person may come to believe in the work ethic as a cornerstone of life.

### Training

Finally, our training and the people who guided us also shape how we see the world. From surgeons to seamstresses and plumbers to potters, most people have spent years in formal and informal apprenticeships, gaining knowledge and expertise. Our teachers, trainers, and mentors, and the subjects they teach, have imprinted specific methods

> *People who are good with hammers see every problem as a nail.*
> **Abraham Maslow**

of problem solving and decision-making that are now our own.

Ruth gives credit to her former academic advisor Dr. Ramirez for grooming her for this job opportunity.

"When I was in graduate school, just after we married, I thought about dropping out and teaching high school. It would have been a lot easier on both of us. I don't know if you remember, John, but I went to Dr. Ramirez and asked his advice. He was aware of my goals, and he also knew I was wavering and thinking of quitting. What he said that day has stuck with me. 'Teaching is a noble calling, but every school from kindergarten to medical school needs to be well run if teachers are to do their jobs. The responsibility to administer and manage schools and universities is also a calling. You bring an uncommon strength of character and intellect, coupled with the breadth of skills necessary for leading a university.'

His words opened a door for me. When I walked through it, the choice influenced the rest of my life. Now, this job could represent the end of my professional journey. When I'm really quiet and ask myself whether to take the offer, I can almost hear Dr. Ramirez's voice. John, I don't want to spend the last years of my working life wondering what might have been."

When we face a difficult choice, we can only do so from our own perspective. Then, we may be able to incorporate other points of view. Sometimes we see things clearly. In other situations, our perspective limits the ability to see and understand what is in front of us. When Ruth reminded John about Dr. Ramirez, she was honoring the rich

> *How hard I find it to see what is right in front of my eyes.*
> **Ludwig Wittgenstein**

perspective—or frame—of her mentor in the field of education. His larger view opened her eyes to possibilities and meanings that were otherwise invisible to her.

## FRAMES AND FRAMING

To create effective decisions, we need ways to simplify and structure all of the information that surrounds us. Good decision-making requires that we maintain focus. Appropriate focus keeps us from being overwhelmed by the tidal wave of information surrounding us. We use the term "frame" to describe how our minds focus and filter our attention. Again, think of the building with many windows. Their frames create our perspectives in several ways.

Frames filter what we take in to help us interact with our world and function in it. Frames help us by setting boundaries that control what is relevant and important or what is irrelevant and less important in the decision-making process. Frames also emphasize or de-emphasize certain aspects by focusing our attention in particular ways. They are the "Swiss army knives" of the mind, all-purpose tools used in every decision we make.

Throughout the book, we will refer to the active process of focusing upon certain facets of a situation and decision as framing. Consider a common decision: how to invest your money in an IRA or other self-managed retirement account. There are thousands of choices, starting with categories of investments such as stocks, bonds, real estate, gold, and so on. Within each category are even more choices. Consider three frames with increasing specificity:

- What stock market investments should I make?
- What stock mutual fund investments should I make?
- What stock market index mutual fund investments should I make?

Each frame helps us limit the decision so it becomes easier to manage. The first frame knocks out bonds and other fixed-income investments. Remaining are thousands of individual stocks and mutual funds. The second frame removes individual stocks from consideration. The last frame removes thousands of mutual funds, leaving only those index funds that offer wide diversification by replicating a stock market index, such as the S & P 500 or the Dow Jones Industrials.

A frame focuses us productively by directing our attention toward what matters to us. It also eliminates other aspects so we can ignore them and avoid wasting time. However, if our frame is too narrow, we fail to consider what might be important and so may reach an inferior decision. Be clear about your decision frame and find the right balance between what is too broad and too narrow. It is not always easy to find this clarity and balance.

A business facing a serious budget shortfall could frame the issue so it contains an important value (caring about our employees' welfare) as a reference point. For example, *"How can we address the $5 million loss in our production operation **without laying off any employees?**"* The value of employee security becomes a major focus, framing the decision sharply and limiting the range of alternatives.

How you pose or frame the question determines your answer. A poor frame reduces the likelihood of a smart choice. In our experience, many poor

> *A problem properly stated is half solved.*
> **John Dewey**

decisions result from the failure to slow down and discuss other people's points of view—that is, the way they frame the situation.

In an organizational environment, participants often frame decisions by applying labels. These categorical descriptions bring some values to the fore and move others out of view. Consider the effect when someone says, *"This is a business decision."* Is this a signal to others that bottom-line financial considerations will rule—that the human element is not part of the mix? In an interdisciplinary team, if the technical members state, *"Fundamentally, this is an engineering decision,"* do the power relationships at the table shift, based on who has this expertise? Some other common labels or categories of decisions include: personnel, strategic, national security, legal, executive, marketing, quality, and moral.

Sometimes we label decisions deliberately. At other times, we do not realize that we, or others, have done so. Either way, labels have two major impacts. First, a label highlights a set of values as primary or core to the decision. These highlighted values often become trump cards that will outweigh other important values. Second, a label identifies appropriate participants. It draws lines that function as boundaries. These boundaries include and exclude people as being relevant to the process, as possible participants at the table, or as being affected by the decision.

*Don't believe everything you think.*
**Popular bumper sticker**

When Ruth tells John, *"Please don't bring my parents into this,"* she may be implicitly framing this decision as an "immediate family decision" instead of an "extended family decision." If so, this frame draws a boundary that leaves extended family members as nonparticipants and, perhaps, excluded from consideration. In white, middle-class North America, with its emphasis on the nuclear family, such a frame is common. In other cultural settings, any decision of significance would be unthinkable without assembling extended family members. In some of these settings, elder members of the extended family network are not only participants but also play a dominant role in shaping the final outcome. Ruth may want to frame out a consideration of the impacts on her parents and siblings. She may feel overwhelmed just considering Sally, John, and her own needs without adding more complexity.

In our work with organizations, families, and individuals, we often encounter another dimension that affects their decisions: the frame of urgency. *"We must make this decision immediately. It can't wait."* A sense of urgency has a dramatic impact on the decision-making process and therefore

*Hasty work, double work.*
**Popular saying**

on the outcome. Urgency usually drives creativity from the process. It may also empower those who are ready to decide, simply because they have already thought about the issue. On the flip side, urgency may limit the influence of those who are relatively new to the issues involved. Finally, urgency limits the opportunity to exchange views and learn from each other. Assumptions usually go untested. There is likely to be little, if any, consideration of what matters to people affected by the decision or consultation of them in advance. People with dominant personalities who want to drive the decision to closure can use urgency as an ally to discourage reflection and deliberation.

In Ruth's case, how long will this offer remain on the table for her to consider? If Preston University pushes her to respond to this major life decision by the end of the week, how will this affect the quality of her deliberations? If they set a deadline, can she negotiate with them for more time so she doesn't have to rush?

## CHANGING FRAMES

Remember that the situation, the decision, and related elements resemble a courtyard surrounded by a multistory building. There are different window frames through which one can view the situation. Perspective shaped by roles, experiences, and training is not fixed. It can change. Sometimes this happens without our effort, as external factors flex or even shatter previous ways of seeing. Major shifts in perspective that cause us to see our world through new eyes are less common than changes that are more modest. However, you may know people who, upon receiving shocking medical news, are jarred into transforming their lives. Similarly, concerted intervention of friends and loved ones has been a catalyst for alcoholics and addicts to own up to their problems and admit they need help.

> *Without our knowing it, we see reality through glasses colored by the subconscious memory or previous experiences.*
> **Thomas Merton**

In less dramatic ways, we can become better decision-makers by looking through another window. Even a modest shift in perspective may provide a clearer view of the situation and what matters.

We are not likely to make the effort to seek out alternative frames if we do not respect their power and usefulness. Most cultures recognize the fundamental connection between the way we see or frame and our ability to understand. Consider these North American sayings:

- "He couldn't see the big picture."
- "You can't see the forest for the trees."
- "She has tunnel vision."
- "He's looking at the world through rose-colored glasses."
- "For him, the glass is always going to be half empty."
- "When life hands you lemons, make lemonade."

- "Hindsight is always twenty-twenty."
- "This is a very short-sighted decision."
- "Keep your eye on the ball."

We see our world through our minds' frames. It is not a question of whether we frame based on our perspective, but how we do so. While frame-free sight is not possible, we can shift perspective and try out different frames. Decisions bounded by frames that fit well simply work better and last longer. When a frame is appropriate and flexible, it can serve us well in managing a challenging, complex situation and help us make a difficult decision. When a frame is rigid, based on flawed assumptions, or limited by our experience, it decreases our ability to make a good decision.

> *Everyone is prone to look for the facts that fit the conclusion they have already reached.*
> **Peter Drucker**

Important choices require that we reach for the best perspective available to us. When we acknowledge that others bring unique perspectives, we benefit. We learn what they see, what is important to them, and what they think should be done. Framing helps focus, sharpen, or shift perspective in order to see the issue and its important elements more clearly.

There are three ways to enhance and expand your frame:

1. **Know your own point of view.** A good decision begins with knowing how you have initially framed the decision. For example, if you see it as a no-win situation, you may fail to see options that minimize losses or uncover possible hidden gains.

2. **Inquire about other perspectives.** If you acknowledge that other perspectives exist and that they are legitimate although different from your own, you lay the foundation for a dialogue that could lead in surprising directions—out of no-win territory into something marginally or even substantially better.

3. **Manage perspective.** Alone or with others, you can move from passively accepting to actively managing frames. Try out different ways of looking at the situation, then experiment with framing a decision in several ways.

With these points in mind, let's return to Ruth and John and the decision facing them at the chapter's beginning.

After the initial rush of excitement and enthusiasm, Ruth stepped back and forced herself to consider the perspectives of John and Sally, her primary stakeholders. In turn, John and Sally tried to think about the move not only in terms of what it would mean for each of them in the near term but also how important it was to Ruth's career—and longer term, what it might mean for Sally's future.

After taking the time to think it over and lowering the emotional heat in family discussions, Ruth found a way to manage perspective and to frame a decision that had the potential to meet the most important needs.

Ruth: "Thanks for helping me out with this. You both know how badly I want this job, and even when you came around to telling me to 'go for it,' I could tell you had reservations. Sally, you're absolutely right—it would be totally unfair to move you away right before your senior year. How about if I propose this to Preston: If I am selected and accept the job, I'll ask them to throw in some on-campus or subsidized housing for twelve months and allow me to work there four days a week for the first year. On the fifth day, I can be available from here via phone and e-mail. That gives me three-day weekends at home. You two stay here until Sally finishes high school, and wherever she goes to college, whether it's Preston or somewhere else with her friends, we'll support that. John, in a way it'll be hardest for you. I hope that during the year you will visit often and we can start planning our transition."

John: "I'm with you Ruth, but I have a condition, too. While you're gone, I don't want to be your parents' prime caregiver. You've got to get your sisters involved and help them begin to plan for the transition as well."

## WHAT YOU CAN DO

### *Know Your Own Perspective*

The goal: Increase your appreciation of the strengths and limits of your personal perspective.

You bring a perspective, no matter the issue. Your effectiveness increases when you become more aware of this point of view, including its strengths and limitations. Right from the start, keep in mind that your perspective is limited and only one of a number of ways to look at the issue. Just by understanding this, you have increased the odds that you will identify the right problem, test assumptions that may be in error, and find the important options.

Retain this awareness throughout the process. At any step along the way, the decision-maker's ability to be self-reflective about the advantages and limitations of her perspective increases the likelihood she will make a good decision.

### Identify the Roles You Play and Their Influence on Your Perspective

How does each role contribute to or limit your ability to understand the issue and think about it carefully?

*"We're not only Sally's parents. We're also the agents of her health and financial security."*

*"More important than my business is my wife's career and happiness. First and foremost, I have to look at this as her husband."*

### Highlight Background Experiences That Shape Your Point of View

*"As an educator, I think of good administration as the foundation for all the other important goals of a college."*

*"You know I have never been particularly receptive to change. I guess it's best after all that you move ahead of me and pave the way."*

### Recognize Possible Blind Spots

Check for parts of the problem that you might not see.

*"What could I be missing as I work through this problem?"*

*"Is there an issue here I'm overlooking? This is a huge challenge. What if I can't do the job? What if there is a change in administration at Preston? I'm basing my decision on the current president and my positive relationship with him."*

*"Do we need a conference with your siblings to weigh in on your parents' well-being?"*

### If You Are on Your Own. . .

Ask yourself similar questions and use the answers to improve your understanding of the decision.

### *Identify and Acknowledge Other Perspectives*

The goal: Benefit from other people's perspectives.

People who take an interest in your decisions, whether at home or at work, will scrutinize and judge you, whether or not they have been involved in making the decision. Even when a decision is yours alone to make, others may need to actively cooperate in making or at least passively accepting the decision. If they do not, implementation may suffer. Effective framing notes other viewpoints and highlights possible concerns, objections, and resistance *before* you commit to a decision and communicate it to others. Views that complement your own can be particularly valuable. They allow you to focus on the decision and prepare to communicate it to others as honestly as possible. When you anticipate others' concerns and points of view, you are in a better position to explain and, if necessary, justify your decision.

### Conduct a Snapshot Round

In a workgroup, a family meeting, or a neighborhood association gathering, before jumping into the issue, ask all the participants to speak briefly to the points of view they bring to the decision. Invite everyone to speak. *"Can we take a few minutes to go around the table and find out what point of view each of us brings to this?"*

Snapshots like this lay the groundwork for improved dialogue as we learn where others are coming from. These initial comments may also highlight underlying assumptions and prejudgments. Snapshot framing doesn't produce a clear statement of the issue to be decided. It simply makes us aware that people may approach the same situation differently.

What people identify in this initial exchange may be very different. Some may immediately identify important values. *"My initial take is that this is a bad idea. We can't disrupt Sally's life, no matter what the advantages are."* Others may jump right to solutions. *"It is absolutely clear what we have to do, and I don't want us to beat around the bush."* Some may identify additional assumptions, feelings, and concerns. *"No matter what I would like to do, I'm pretty much stuck as my parents' caregiver. Once again my sisters leave me holding the bag."*

### Acknowledge How People See the Situation Differently

*"It helps me think about this if I realize that there are a number of very different and valid ways to look at this question."* Conversations about values-laden issues can heat up quickly. Acknowledgment is powerful and keeps the climate respectful, encouraging everyone to speak up.

*"Stop! You just dumped this huge issue on the table that you have already thought about. It may look great to you, but I need you to take some time to look at this through my eyes."*

### Be on the Lookout for Decision "Gold"

Sometimes valuable nuggets hide in people's early comments about their points of view. If something significant pops up early, note it in some way so you can come back to it later. For example:

- **Important values** to discuss in more detail later: *"I would like to hear from everyone first, but let's make sure we come back to John's comment about my parents. I think we need to talk that through carefully."*

- **Possible solutions** to be considered at the appropriate time: *"Before we move to solutions, can we talk more about what's important to all of you? Then, when we're ready to consider options we can start with Sally's idea."*

- **Essential participants** who are missing and need to be involved: *"Ruth, I know this is our decision, but I want you to consider the role your sisters can and should play. Will we reach a better decision if we involve them now?"*

**If You are on Your Own. . .**

If you don't hear from others about their different perspectives, you must find a way to gain this awareness on your own. This is a serious challenge, because each of us is, to some degree, a prisoner of his or her own perspective. Push yourself to consider others who may care about this issue. *"How will others see this differently from me? What can I do to benefit from different perspectives as I come to a decision?"*

## Frame the Decision You Must Make

The goal: Articulate a clear, focused description of the issue you will be deciding.

Important decisions require careful, sometimes lengthy, framing activity. One of our clients described the deliberate framing work he did as the inspector general of a large government agency. When a new request for an investigation came in, he and his staff spent the first week carefully describing the nature of the investigation and its scope. They framed the question that would be investigated and attempted to clarify what it included and what it excluded. This was far more than pushing words around on a piece of paper. His experience convinced him that careful attention to framing at the beginning usually saved time, energy, and misery. There are endless examples of individuals, groups, and organizations solving the wrong problem, going off half-cocked, or failing to consider important aspects of a situation before acting.

### Define the Issue for Decision and Put It in Writing

*"If we try to craft the decision we must make by stating it as a question to be answered, how would we say it?"*

Consider how others have posed questions or defined similar problems. *"Didn't Joe's company face a similar issue recently before the city council? Should we give him a call and find out how he dealt with the open-space requirements of the ordinance in his presentation?"*

Make sure there is clarity about the basic framework for the decision:

- Whose decision is this?
- When must the decision be made?
- Who should be involved and consulted before the decision is made?

### Limit the Decision

Consider emphasis. *"As we have initially framed this, what does our frame highlight?"*

Be clear about what is excluded. *"What does our frame leave out?"*
Identify labels. *"What kind of an issue is this?"*

### Identify Assumptions

*"Are we making any assumptions here?"*
*"If so, what steps do we need to take to test them so we are on solid ground with our decision?"*

### If You are on Your Own. . .

Ask yourself similar questions and use the answers to clarify your understanding of the decision.

See the "Worksheet for Step 1: Clarify Perspective" in the Appendix.

## Remember:

- Fight the natural urge to plunge in "frame blind." Don't rush to a decision.
- Recognize that we make mistakes in both directions. We can frame too narrowly and fail to consider important stakeholders and their values, or we can frame too broadly and bog down with too much information.
- Come back to framing as needed. *"I'm not so sure we are looking at this in the best way. What if we considered it from a different angle?"*

## Consider another story about a controversial community issue. . . .

In a meeting open to the public, a community library board is considering what to do. As you read the story, ask yourself the following questions.

- What are the different points of view in this situation?
- What assumptions do any of these perspectives contain?
- Who else, not yet identified, might be affected by this decision?

> Board Chair: "Thank you for coming out tonight and sharing your comments with our library board. Let me summarize what I've heard. The Protect Our Children (POC) group has asked that our newly donated computers be equipped with filters and that we limit Internet access. POC wants to protect minors from offensive Internet content (pornography, violence, bigotry) and from potentially harmful chat room contact with sexual predators. They believe we have a duty to the children of our community and to families. The Friends of Civil Liberties chapter has raised concerns about censorship and civil rights. Their members strongly oppose any limitations on access. They believe that any restrictions on access to information are suspect and must be avoided. Joan Wilson, representing the American Library Association, has submitted their code of ethics that supports freedom of access to information. She has also included a list of concerns about the proper role of library staff as information providers, not enforcement personnel.

As board chair I want to thank Computer Enterprises for their generous donation which, for the first time, will let us fully equip our library with up-to-date computers. I am concerned that both POC and Friends of Civil Liberties have already stated their intention to pursue formal political and legal action if we do not honor their concerns. I hope the board can, at its next meeting on Thursday at 4 p.m., come to a resolution that works for our community as a whole. We'll inform you of our decision at our next public meeting and will entertain any questions you might have about the board's deliberations."

# 2

## Comprehend What Matters

*Our lives begin to end the day we become silent about things that matter.*

Martin Luther King Jr.

### MURDER OR MERCY?

Julie Latham and her thirty-five-year-old husband planned to celebrate their tenth wedding anniversary hiking in the Colorado Rockies. However, while packing for the long-awaited trip, Rick Latham suddenly collapsed. The emergency room physicians diagnosed a rapidly progressing brain infection, and within three days, Rick lost consciousness. In an instant, the couple's bright future irreversibly shifted course.

Rick lay in a coma connected to "life" by a ventilator and feeding tube. As she sat at his bedside day and night, Julie realized that Rick was dying. As his medical/legal decision-maker she faced a painful prospect. Fortunately, they had discussed their wishes and signed the necessary paperwork. However, who of us—really—imagines using such a document? On top of the stress of losing her husband, Julie was out of patience with Rick's neurologist, Dr. Rall. Whenever she approached him to discuss the issue of stopping the life support treatment, he brushed her off. He never seemed to have time for her.

Four weeks later, after a particularly draining and despairing day, Julie confronted Dr. Rall in the hallway. "I've told you and told you," she said, "that I'm speaking for Rick now, and I have the legal say-so to prove it." She waved her durable power of attorney for health care form in Dr. Rall's face. "I have the right to make medical decisions for Rick, I know what he wants, and if you don't stop treatment today, I'll see you in court."

Dr. Rall paused and faced Julie, his eyes as cold and steely as his voice. "That's your privilege, Mrs. Latham, but I'm not in the practice of murdering my patients."

*****

The year was 1983, and this was the hospital ethics committee's first consult. End-of-life decisions made national headlines, and durable powers of attorney for health care remained largely untested. The hospital chaplain asked several members of the ethics committee, including the hospital's risk manager, to meet with her, Mrs. Latham, and Dr. Rall to deepen the discussion. The committee chair scheduled a meeting for Tuesday afternoon at 4:30 p.m.

Chapter 1 showed how personal perspective points each of us in a certain direction and orients our initial approach to an issue or decision. When people speak with strength and passion, it is clear that something really matters. Strong statements signal the presence of underlying values.

This story begins with two powerful and seemingly opposing perspectives. Julie Latham is the one with the emotional investment in her husband's life (and death), and she believes her only recourse is obtaining control through the law. Dr. Rall claims what he perceives as the absolute, moral high road.

> *There are no misunderstandings; there are only failures to communicate.*
> **Senagalese Proverb**

It is natural for the intensity of opening statements to shape the terms of the exchange, leaving embedded values unexamined—and thus we risk missing what is really important. A strong opening often conceals as much as it reveals. If the process stops here, we remain blind to other values. Situations are usually more complicated and nuanced than any single person can fully appreciate. We need to push past the limited terms of engagement. If we explore, listen, and add to the list of things that matter, we are more likely to gain new and surprising insights about others and ourselves.

In this chapter, we describe three ways to learn, go deeper into what matters, and better understand the full range of values at work:

1. Establish useful background information by understanding **context**
2. Discover what matters by **naming** values
3. Share stories through **dialogue.**

## UNDERSTANDING CONTEXT

Every decision we face is situated. It arrives at a certain time, in a particular place. As we saw in the previous chapter, we are cast in specific roles and bring unique histories, experiences, preferences, and predispositions. Tough choices speak to each of us in ways no one else can understand unless we tell them.

As the conversation about values expands, so must the exploration of important background information. Values come to life only when we place them in a current and concrete setting. When we take the time to speak our history and experience, we become clearer about what really matters, and why.

Sometimes we are blind to what pushes and pulls us. Good decision-making, whether personal or professional, solo or in a group, requires that we ask pointed questions to lay bare contextual features that influence the decision.

> *When the chips are down, meaning is negotiated: you slowly figure out what you have in common, what it is safe to talk about, how you can communicate unshared experience or create a shared vision. With enough flexibility in bending your world view and with luck and skill and charity, you may achieve some mutual understanding.*
> **George Lakoff and Mark Johnson**

- Who are the people and groups the decision may affect?
- Beyond awareness of the roles we play, what can we say about the roles' demands and what they mean to us in this situation?
- How do preexisting relationships influence our behavior and the conversation?
- What values do we bring from personal experience, professional expectations, and cultural influences?

Failure to bring these contextual elements from background to foreground leaves that elephant in the middle of the room: no amount of eloquent or contentious conversation dislodges the elephant. Unspoken realities often trump all other considerations unless we call them out.

Julie Latham came to the table under circumstances most of us would call tragic. She was a wife whose vigorous young husband was dying unexpectedly. She was also a lawyer and public defender, comfortable with advocacy and making legal arguments. Dr. Rall arrived as a physician, nearing the end of his career. He was struggling to adjust to the new population of patients and families demanding to make their own medical decisions. Dr. Rall and Mrs. Latham met for the first time in the ICU. They had no relationship or understanding of how to work together. The hospital's risk manager was new to his job and understood clearly the hospital administrator's expectation: protect our hospital, our staff, and our patients. The

> *The silly question is the first intimation of some totally new development.*
> **Alfred North Whitehead**

chaplain saw similar dilemmas daily and was skilled at starting better conversations. Her question to herself was, *"How can I help Mrs. Latham and Dr. Rall discover, together, what is really important?"*

There are always actors who bring history and experience, play certain roles, and behave accordingly. The situation is often complicated and rich. To get our arms around this complexity, we need each other. Together, we can fill in the spaces between us and the blind spots around us and also create a clear picture of what matters, and why.

The chaplain acknowledged Mrs. Latham's legal claim. "Our committee has begun to discuss the new state law allowing surrogate decision makers to make end-of-life decisions. This is an important area for us, as well as for you. We need to learn how to do this better. You can help us with this. In addition to this legal issue, is there anything else that is important for you?"

Mrs. Latham hesitated. "From the moment he collapsed, Rick and I knew something was terribly wrong. Some months ago, following my mother's death, we drew up living wills and durable health care power of attorney forms for both of us. We hadn't signed them. I brought Rick's from home, and he signed the papers the day before he lost consciousness. I know it's legal and binding, but. . . this is hard. After he signed, Rick said, 'Promise me one thing. If it doesn't go well, don't waste our modest savings on treatment that doesn't work. Just stop. I'm not afraid of death. I'm afraid of dying that just goes on and on. I don't want that for me. I don't want that for you.' I promised. I know I have the legal responsibility for making this decision. It's devastating. Can you imagine how painful it would be for me if the last thing I do for Rick is break my promise?"

> *It is not hard to make decisions when you know what your values are.*
> **Roy Disney**

Silence fell as Mrs. Latham put her head down and wept. Next, it was Dr. Rall's turn. The chaplain asked him to explain more about his position, how he had handled similar cases in the past, and what mattered to him in Rick Latham's case. He waited for some time and then said, "It's not that I don't ever stop life support treatment. I do. My wife died last year, and I made the decision to turn off her ventilator. I may very well get to that point with Mr. Latham. It's just that, more and more, I'm expected to do whatever anyone demands. What really bothers me is the wall of distrust that is growing between physicians, patients, and families. It is especially painful when we're facing end-of-life decisions and should be working together. When I turn off a ventilator, no matter how right the decision, it's as if a piece of my soul dies. I'm not an especially religious man, but for me it's a sacred moment, beyond law and hospital policy. That's what matters to me. Does anyone care?"

The risk manager confirmed that Mrs. Latham's paperwork seemed to be in order and aligned with the new state law. "I must admit, however, that authorizing someone else to discontinue life support still worries me. We don't have a specific hospital policy on how to do this. My job is to protect the hospital from lawsuits."

How different from and more meaningful than the initial conflict: "It's my legal right and I'll sue you if you don't comply," and "I don't murder my patients!"

## NAMING WHAT MATTERS

The heart of the matter is often different from our initial statements and beliefs. We misread the situation. We misread others. Sometimes, we misread ourselves. The best way to go deeper is to talk it through. We must *name* what, for us, really matters, explain what it means and why. We also must challenge ourselves to listen to others who have a stake in the outcome.

> *We have two ears and a mouth so that we can listen twice as much as we speak.*
> **Epictetus**

A forum designed to reduce heat and shed light can help. The ethics committee provided a place and opportunity for Mrs. Latham and Dr. Rall to speak, listen to, and learn from each other. Remember: no one except the person holding a value can speak with authority about its personal meaning to him or her.

Sometimes a decision requires group discussion. At other times, a decision-maker may be working alone. Whether or not the decision involves a group, and even when the decision seems to be the business of only one person, others invariably are affected. Their perspectives are important early on, as the decision takes shape. The issue is not an insistence on group consensus or a softhearted concern for the needs of others. Rather, it is a hardheaded assessment that decisions improve when we take steps to engage those who have a stake in the outcome.

Of course, adding more people to the discussion invites more values and concerns. The initial effect may be confusion and conflict. In the end, welcoming divergent positions can strengthen a difficult and controversial decision. Critics often base their disapproval on the failure to identify and respect what matters to others, especially those who disagree. Good decisions, decisions that last and that work, do not satisfy everyone. Those who make such

> *When you encounter difficulties and contradictions, do not try to break them, but bend them with gentleness and time.*
> **St. Frances de Sales**

good decisions do, however, seriously consider and acknowledge the range of values important to all those involved.

Resolving the apparent conflict between Mrs. Latham and Dr. Rall, and deciding on next steps, turned out to be quite simple. First, they needed a forum where they could speak and be heard. Then they needed some help in talking about the issue in a new way. The chaplain invited them to go beneath their initial position and discover what else mattered. When they arrived at *"I must keep my last promise to my husband"* and *"For me, stopping life support treatment is a sacred moment,"* everyone around the table knew that Mrs. Latham and Dr. Rall had moved beyond their impasse and arrived at the heart of the matter.

> As the meeting ended, Mrs. Latham and Dr. Rall began talking directly to each other. "What I propose is the following. There are two more tests I want to run, to rule out the possibility of a reversible condition. Your husband is young; his body is strong. I should have the results by the end of this week, and if nothing positive shows up, then I agree. It's time to stop treatment. Can you go along with that?"
>
> Mrs. Latham sat back in her chair and took a deep breath before answering, "I can."

The assertion of what we want often involves the exchange of positions or the lodging of demands. This level of conversation easily breaks down into a power struggle. When Julie Latham asserted her legal rights, Dr. Rall countered by characterizing her desire as murder. Only by moving beyond *what* to do and naming *why* this matters to us can we leave the territory of power and begin the journey to the heart of the matter.

## DEEPENING THE CONVERSATION

Even when people bring values into the conversation by naming them, there is more to do. Most values talk is like an oil slick that remains on the surface of the water: it shimmers but shares little chemistry with the many layers of meaning that flow underneath. Superficial values talk can also be toxic to the deeper, vital understandings that are possible.

> *Conversation is thinking in its natural state.*
> **Malvina Reynolds**

Three common patterns of values talk keep the exchange at this surface layer of meaning. First, we can have make-nice discussions without understanding that important words like safety, quality, excellence, and integrity mean different things to each of us in certain situations. Second, we can have passionate debate with vigorous point/counterpoint that produces heat but little light. Third, there is dead-end conversation that bogs down under the weight of the values, causing frustration or confusion.

The solution is to go deeper. Penetrating the oil slick requires that we leave the realm of conversation or debate and enter into dialogue. Formed from the Latin root words *dia* and *logos*, dialogue denotes the exchange of meaning through the spoken word. Dialogue flows among people through a process of shared inquiry, respectful listening, and reflection upon what we say and what we hear. Its goal is mutual understanding, not victory or

## Dimensions of Values Conversation

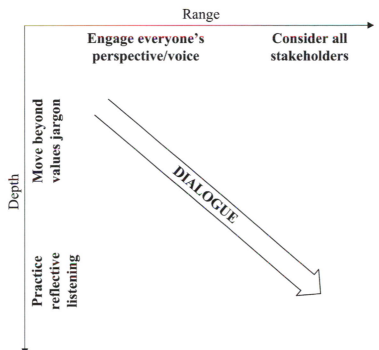

supremacy; its attitude is collaborative, not adversarial. Dialogue assumes that together we hold the pieces necessary for good decisions.

To move toward dialogue, we must first break the destructive habit of speaking in serial monologues. Typically, when someone is speaking in a charged exchange about an important decision, others are not listening but waiting to speak. They are waiting to make a point, rehearsing what they want to say, or mentally critiquing the speaker's point. All of these natural activities undermine the exchange of meaning that is critically important for communicating values effectively. Participants speak in isolation. People's statements remain disconnected, and no one listens well.

Values words are shorthand code for powerful and intensely personal interests and beliefs. For each of us, the real story of a value like integrity or justice lies deep beneath the surface. The reasons why something matters in a given situation are usually not obvious. It takes intention, some skill, and courage to go beneath what we might first proclaim most important and decipher the code.

> *I wouldn't give a fig for simplicity on this side of complexity, but I would give my life for simplicity on the other side of complexity.*
> **Oliver Wendell Holmes**

Who can disagree with: *"Respect one another," "Do no harm," "Keep promises," "Be fair," "Be loyal," "Be a good steward?"* If such formal values language is called for, it should start, not stop or highjack a conversation. Unless someone explains what he or she means by respect, harm, fairness, loyalty, or stewardship in a particular situation, invoking jargon offers little in the way of practical guidance. It also can cause others to retreat into silence, become defensive and resistant, or fire back in hostile disagreement.

> Four days later, with family and close friends standing with her at the bedside, Julie Latham watched while Dr. Rall withdrew her husband's life support. Rick Latham died five minutes later. Julie asked everyone to leave so she could be alone with Rick's body. When she emerged an hour later, Dr. Rall was waiting in the hall, working on patient charts. He stood and walked to her side. Taking her hands in his he said, "I want you to know that your loyalty to Rick's wishes and your courage in facing all of this touched many of us who work here. Rick would be very proud of you."

## WHAT YOU CAN DO

### *Unpack the Context*

The goal: Explore the roles, relationships, history, and experience that make otherwise abstract values personal and immediate.

All decision-making is local, practical, and concrete. Abstract values come alive when you describe their roots in your personal history and experience. *"My wife died of cancer last year, and I had to decide when to stop life support treatment."* When you isolate issues from their personal, historical, and cultural origins, you often fail to grasp their lived meaning for real people facing real choices. *"I understand that it is my responsibility to make medical decisions for my husband. It's devastating."* You may feel more comfortable keeping the conversation formal and conceptual. *"State law respects my autonomy and gives me the right to execute a durable power of attorney for health care on behalf of my husband."*

Up close and personal revelations can bring a certain amount of risk and discomfort. *Silence fell as Mrs. Latham put her head down and wept. "Does anyone care?"* Conversation that remains at the level of abstract values words may feel safer. Rarely is it real. Instead, avoid big values words and formal, abstract language about principles and core values. What you mean, what you can explain in concrete terms, is what matters.

### Honor Your Role(s)

Recognize the various roles you play. Each has its own voice and evokes a set of values, sometimes quite insistently. You are the sum of your roles, virtually assuring conflict within you and with others. Start by understanding the roles you bring to the table and acknowledging the values important to each one. Then determine what, in this situation, is to be your leading role.

*"In this situation I'm speaking not as an attorney but as a wife, and what matters to me is. . . ."*

*"I'm a physician, and I have professional duties to my patients and my profession."*

*"As risk manager my job is to minimize legal exposure for our hospital."*

*"My purpose here is to help the two of you find a way forward, together if possible."*

### Reveal Your Roots

The first step is to understand and communicate what influences you. Discuss your history as it affects your perspective and values. Helping others understand why you see things as you do does not have to take much time. *"My wife died last year from pancreatic cancer."*

Acknowledge relationships, personal experience, and cultural values that influence your positions and priorities. *"My mother came from a generation that didn't talk about death. Rick and I were determined to talk with each other and make plans ahead of time."*

You must navigate and manage the traditions, expectations, and taboos of the various groups to which you belong: family, gender, community, organization, profession, faith community, country of origin. You live cross-cultural lives where values compete and often insist that you choose them over others. *"I admit it's hard for me to put aside the fact that you're a lawyer. As a physician, it's always in the back of my mind when we talk."*

### Peel the Onion

Explore what lies beyond your initial perspective. More important than "what" is "why."

*"Rick and I promised each other we would ease the burden of decision-making as much as possible. That's why this document is so important to me."*

To help others, use open questions that invite the speaker to go deeper.

*"Would you be willing to tell us more about autonomy and why it is so important to you?"*

*"What is it about promise-keeping that makes it so critical. Whose promises matter most if not all can be honored?"*

*"Could you say more about 'do no harm' in this situation?"*

Digging deep brings you close the core of your identity, to a place where you feel most vulnerable. When you explain what matters to you, candidly and without artifice, your values come alive for others and rarely need further explication. *"I can't imagine that the last thing I would do to Rick is break a promise."*

### If You are on Your Own. . .

Without others to speak to about roles, roots, and what lies beneath initial importance, you must interview yourself. Ask these questions:

- What roles do I play in this situation?
- What does each role require of me?
- Is there one role that is dominant or leading?
- What else influences me in this situation (relationships, experience, culture)?
- What seems to be important and why?

### *Learn What Matters*

The goal: Build a comprehensive list of what matters to all stakeholders and negotiate a common understanding of these values.

Make time and space for clear statements of, *"What is important here?"* High-quality decisions begin with early and continuous focus on people's values, no matter what the topic or venue. Skilled decision-makers know their own values and can explain them to others. They know how to elicit and listen carefully to what matters to others who have a stake in the decision. They seek out more, not fewer, stakeholders.

### Ask Discovery Questions

Ask people, *"What seems to be important here?"* or *"Who cares about this issue and what matters to them?"* or *"If the morning newspaper were to run an article about this decision and how we approached it, what would they say?"*

Because people often invoke the same value to argue for radically different behaviors, you need to be precise about what someone means. When someone names a value, ask for specifics.

*"So it's about trustworthiness. Can you tell me more about the circumstances here that raise this issue for you?"*

*"When you say autonomy, do you mean you should have the right to make your own medical decisions?"*

*"What would help me understand this better from your perspective?"*

See the "Asking the Right Questions" worksheet in the Appendix.

## Close the Loop

Check for accuracy and let the speaker know you have listened well. Communication succeeds when a listener reflects back to the speaker what she has heard and then has it confirmed. *"Let me make sure I understand. Your durable power of attorney for health care gives you authority to make end-of-life decisions for your husband, and you want that authority respected."*

If you are in a group, write down what people say to keep track of their points and honor their voice. Use a flip chart or white board to keep the values in front of everyone for consideration throughout the discussion. *"Could we stop and capture some of the key points people have made so far? I want to make sure that we keep them in mind when it's time to consider options."*

When you take time to reflect and clarify what others say, you show them you have listened, not merely waited your turn to speak. People whose values are respected, even if their values do not carry the day, are less likely to sabotage a decision later on. *"I know you may not agree with me, but I appreciate you taking the time to hear me out."*

## Stay Curious

Check assumptions often and resist the temptation to close out the conversation prematurely. *"Should we check with someone from the legal department to make sure we understand the regulation?"*

Faced with difficult issues and tense exchanges, it is tempting to jump immediately to problem solving. This can short-circuit the learning phase and weaken a decision's foundation. *"What else are we missing here?"*

Seek out the quiet participants. *"There are some of you who haven't spoken. I'd like to hear from you about what's important."*

If time permits and the decision warrants, conduct a careful and thorough stakeholder values analysis: *"Have we consulted or considered everyone who will be affected? Have we heard from them about what matters?"*

*"Should we meet with Mrs. Latham and her family separately? Perhaps a more private forum would help them express the full range of their concerns."*

## If You are on Your Own. . .

Pay attention to stakeholders and assumptions. Though the decision is yours alone, consider how your decision will affect others. Then do your best to identify what matters to individuals and groups who connect to the situation and your decision. *"If Rick's brothers could be here with me, what would they want for Rick and me?"*

Pay particular attention to assumptions. It is easy to overlook them as they often lie beneath our awareness, where they remain untested. *"If Rick knew the terrible bind I'm in because of my promise to him, would he really want me to carry it out?"*

### Promote Dialogue

The goal: Speak and listen in a way that opens you to be changed by what someone else says.

Skilled decision-makers understand that early and open dialogue is a valuable investment of time and energy. The investment does not always provide an immediate return, but over time, the benefits can be substantial. Talking and listening only to ourselves or to our inner circle of trusted advisors will not give us the depth or scope of understanding we need. You must dig deeper into what others believe is important. You need to pay attention to diverse positions and solicit participation from people who have a stake in the issue, especially when they disagree with you. By doing so, you make stronger and clearer decisions. Decision-makers pay a price for not involving people affected by the decision. Stakeholders who remain out of the loop are more likely to be harshly critical and prone to undermine a decision once it is made.

### Harness the Power of Stories

Recognize that "facts" do not exist without interpretation. Humans are hardwired to be storytellers. They tell stories to find direction, make sense of a situation, and get their bearings.

Invite people to share some of the story behind their values. *"What can you tell me about the road that brought you to your conclusion?"*

Resist the temptation to tell someone else's story for them. *"I don't want to put words in your mouth. Please tell me more."*

Pay attention to who the different narrators are, what point of view each takes, what they select as important information, and how they order events. *"Dr. Rall, we have heard from Mrs. Latham. Tell us how you see what's happened so far and what you'd like to do next."*

Invite people to connect and merge their stories. *"Now that you have heard directly from each other, how do you see the differences that brought you here?"*

### Look for Common Ground

Use stories to locate areas of agreement or a degree of positive resonance. Conflicts highlight differences. Telling and listening to stories is an effective way to defuse tension and negotiate common understanding when differences seem insurmountable. You are more likely to understand someone else, especially when conflict and feelings are intense, if you offer your own story and others invite you into theirs. *"My wife died last year, and I too was faced with a difficult decision. I've experienced this personally as well as professionally. Let me tell you what I propose for us to do, together, for your husband. Please tell me what you think."*

*"I am clear about where we disagree, but I wonder where we might agree."*

### Walk, Don't Run

Think of decisions that fail or need serious, after-the-fact revision. How much does the "fix" cost in terms of time, energy, and resources? How much money, not to mention grief, can a decision-maker save by listening carefully and thoroughly, early on, to all those who have a stake in the decision and its outcome?

A sense of urgency pervades daily life. Today's decisions need to be made yesterday. There is no time to have a thoughtful discussion about what is important, let alone consult with important stakeholders. Just the bottom line, please. Many of these emergencies are perceived but artificial. Successful negotiators understand that if you want to maintain the status quo, rush the process.

Slow down the conversation. Ask for explanations. *"Say more about that, if you can."* Resist the imperative to decide quickly. If you want to explore different points of view and perhaps shift the balance of power, slow things down. *"Are we missing anything here?"*

*"Shall we go away for a bit and think about this?"*

*"Should we bring others to the table before we go further?"*

Develop a comfort with silence. Breathe and count slowly to ten, if necessary. Meaning and understanding often grow better in the spaces between people and their sentences. Not all cultures suffer from speech behavior patterns that rush to fill gaps in the conversation.

For those who like to stay on task, this step may seem uncontrolled and chaotic. It may appear to be a colossal waste of time because it is exploratory and not immediately linked to options and choices. Our position is clear: expand the complexity before homing in on potential solutions. When you slow down and let this step unfold, your decisions are more likely to work well. They will last longer and enjoy more widespread support than decisions made on the fly and in isolation.

### Check for the Elephant in the Room

Differences and disagreements are real, as is the reluctance to raise or respond to them in conversation with others. Especially when a speaker's language projects accusation and blame about unfairness, historic injustice, or painful prejudice, you may find yourself at a loss as to what to say. Sometimes people invoke differences because they care about them deeply. At other times, they use them to manipulate. Whether the intent is genuine or tactical, those on the receiving end retreat into defensiveness or hostile silence.

Make space for people to speak directly to differences. Take a breath and take it seriously. If you greet differences with curiosity instead of judgment, you leave room for everyone to move forward.

If the issue involves the past, pull a chair to the table for history. Leave an empty chair available. It can serve as a powerful reminder of the presence of the unspoken, giving permission to raise difficult, even painful issues relating to personal experiences and injustices while keeping the tone respectful.

### Deal with Problematic Conduct

People can be unreasonable, rigid, disrespectful, or abusive. For dialogue to work, people must be willing to respond and listen. What can you do when people behave in challenging, obstructive ways?

- Focus on behavior. Find the best time and place to raise the issue, remembering that confronting someone about his or her behavior, in front of others, can trigger defensiveness or aggression that make matters worse. Balance firmness with respect. *"John, I have a concern about your referring to the Walker family as 'those people.' You may not intend it this way, but it implies to me that you see them as less important than other families we see here in the hospital. I request that you avoid this term and refer to them by name."*

- Set a boundary. Sometimes firm and respectful requests are not enough. People persist in offensive and difficult behavior. Be clear about what isn't acceptable to you. Then, as a warning, not a threat, commit to what will happen if they violate the boundary. *"Mrs. Jones, I am willing to listen to you and do my best to respond to your concerns. I am clear that you are angry with my staff about what happened. However, it is not acceptable to me that you call them a bunch of lying jerks. If you call them names again, I will end the meeting and leave the room."*

- Walk away with respect. In difficult situations, you need to know when to say, *"Enough."* Respectful withdrawal may be the wisest course when you have made serious efforts to address differences and find yourself at a dead end instead of a bridge. Remember that timing matters. If you walk away without judgment or an angry explosion, there may be another opportunity, at a better time, when progress is possible. *"Mr. Lacey, I find myself out of ideas and out of patience with our discussion, which seems to be going nowhere. I think I understand your concerns and I sense you have given me a fair hearing. Our beliefs about what is fair are just so far apart. I am going to call it a day. I don't think we have anything else to talk about unless one of us has a new idea about how to come together."*

### If You are on Your Own. . .

Although dialogue in the true sense involves two or more people, our inner conversation is real. *"I'm of two minds about this question. Part of me wants to just get it over with, but I know I need to be patient."*

Slow down and find a way to capture the messages from inside. Use a journal or record your different voices as they speak to the issue at hand. Then take the time to review these different perspectives. Note what seems to have weight or significance.

### Remember:

• Speak directly and concretely to each other about what you mean, what you value, and why.
• Keep the forum and dialogue respectful and safe for all participants.
• Be open and generous with your own story.

See "Worksheet for Step 2: Comprehend What Matters" in the Appendix.

### Consider another story, this one a difficult personnel issue.

As you read the following story, ask yourself:

• Questions of context: Who is involved and what are their roles? What history might be important? Can you imagine some of the personal experiences that may shape how different people view this issue?
• Story questions: If asked what matters to them, how might each of those involved answer? What stories might people tell to explain their values and bring them to life?

"Thank you all for clearing time for this meeting. As you know, the personnel issue with Sean has heated up, and I need to make a decision about his future with our library. While it's ultimately my decision as library director, I want you, as members of my management team, on board with my decision. Let me review where we are. Sean Randall has worked as a librarian for this community library for twenty-three years. He has an outstanding employment record, has received two merit awards, and always has gone above and beyond, coming in at night and on weekends to pick up slack for other employees who needed help.

Two years ago Sean was diagnosed with chronic fatigue syndrome. This is a disease about which we know little. It may be caused by a virus. What we do know is that there is no known cure and it can be partially or totally incapacitating. As of today, Sean's used all of the sick leave and vacation time available. His productivity has fallen off significantly. We've authorized a temporary abbreviated schedule for Sean, but even then, he has made a number of significant mental errors—errors that have cost our library time, staff energy, and money to correct. Sean's coworkers are losing patience. While some encourage me to 'stick with Sean,' others complain about overwork and the appearance of preferential treatment. With Sean's permission, I've spoken with his physicians. They cannot give us any prognosis that permits hope that he will ever improve.

As you all know, Sean is a single parent, the sole source of support for two teenage children, one of whom hopes to go to college next fall. Sean has no disability insurance coverage. He chose the maximum take-home pay option to meet the family's immediate needs and to set aside money for his children's college expenses. I promised Sean I'd make a decision by the end of this week. Help me think this through."

# 3

## Commit to What Matters Most

*Ideals are like stars; you will not succeed in touching them with your hands, but like the seafaring man on the desert of waters, you choose them as your guides, and following them, you reach your destiny.*

Carl Schurz

When we switch off a light at night, it takes our eyes a minute or two to adjust to the darkness. If we leave a lighted room and step outside, chances are we can't spot the North Star or a favorite constellation right off the bat. The first bright star we see will eventually recede into a maze of glitter. Then, as our eyes adjust, we begin to orient ourselves. So it is with decision-making. As our emotions shift and our minds adjust, we take time to focus on the important values, those with steady luminescence. These are stars by which we can navigate. These values go to the heart of our decision.

The previous chapter urged us to explore what matters to stakeholders. When we dig deeper, the complexity of the values picture emerges. We hear the ticking of the decision-making clock and realize that we can't please everyone or honor every important value. Here is where it is essential to resist the urge to rush to a swift and superficial conclusion. Instead, we must pause to assess all that we've discovered in our investigation. This is our opportunity to focus on a few values that have the greatest weight—the guiding values that will orient our decision-making.

This chapter describes the third challenge on the road to a good decision: determining what matters most and committing to it. Since this step often involves the painful process of choosing, not between right and wrong, but between right and right, we proceed with a foot gently resting on the brake pedal, ready to slow things down if necessary.

## HEALTH INSURANCE: FOR SOME OR ALL?

Integrated Maintenance Solutions (IMS) is a large interstate company that provides contract services for commercial office buildings—everything from janitorial to landscaping, plumbing to roofing. Like many employers, it offers health insurance coverage as a benefit to full-time employees. Every year, during the annual enrollment period, employees have the opportunity to choose between two plans, each offered by a different insurance company.

Six weeks ago, Jane Blaisdell, the CEO of IMS, received a letter from Geneco Health Plan, one of their health providers. Geneco is considering excluding certain conditions from coverage or increasing the premium per employee to maintain existing coverage. Geneco has asked IMS for comments before issuing its revised plan.

Because she always consults employees about proposed changes in their benefits package, Ms. Blaisdell appointed a team of three senior managers, headed by Theresa Gomez, director of human resources, to investigate Geneco's proposal, seek employee opinions, and send her a recommendation about how to proceed. The team also includes Jerry Rinaldi, chief financial officer and John Wallace, marketing director.

The team will, of course, check perspective, listen well, and invite employees to generate their list of values and concerns. The temptation to rush a decision may be strongest at this point, even if up to now we have resisted the urge to decide with dispatch. The first two steps we've described—clarify perspective and comprehend what matters—expand our knowledge by identifying stakeholders, acknowledging their unique perspectives, and listing their concerns and interests. As we end the expanding part of the journey and begin to narrow our scope by prioritizing values, the desire to accelerate to a final decision can be irresistible.

This chapter describes an important shift in direction and urges patience as we turn toward commitment. Here we learn to probe for **deep knowledge**, highlight **competing goods**, and identify the **guiding values** against which to test

> *Anything less than a conscious commitment to the important is an unconscious commitment to the unimportant.*
> **Stephen Covey**

possible solutions. Clear and effective decisions emerge from conscious choice and commitment to what is most important.

### DEEP KNOWLEDGE

After the IMS team listened to employees, they began to explore the issue in depth.

Theresa: "One of our employees, Ruby Romero, has Gaucher's disease. It's not curable, but it is manageable with a very expensive drug. Depending on her dosage, the annual cost runs $300,000–$400,000. Without this drug, she'll likely die within eighteen months. She's a fifty-two-year-old widow with two adult children, and she's been a loyal employee for twenty-two years. Unfortunately, Gaucher's disease is on the list of conditions Geneco proposes to exclude by rider. Within the present enrollment period, Ruby will exhaust the lifetime allowable coverage ($1,000,000) in her current plan (the alternative to Geneco). That plan has just rewritten its policy to exclude her and cases like hers from now on. In this year's open enrollment, Ruby's only hope of remaining insured is to go with Geneco if it covers her condition."

Jerry: "The other side of the coin is that as an alternative to restricting coverage, Geneco proposes to increase employees' monthly premiums by $50 per month for the upcoming year. That's almost a 20 percent increase!"

> *I don't know what the key to success is, but the key to failure is trying to please everyone.*
> **Bill Cosby**

John: "This could also turn into a giant public relations issue. Not three weeks ago the newspaper ran a feature on health insurance that stressed the challenges for workers with rare and expensive conditions. The reporter interviewed Mrs. Romero, who commented at length on her health situation. With all that publicity, whatever we decide will wind up in the paper, particularly if Mrs. Romero loses her coverage. Theresa, are there any other employee issues on the table?"

Theresa: "The human resources division conducted extensive surveys and focus groups with employees about their health benefits preferences, given the relative cost of different benefit packages. Overall, employee opinion clearly indicates that a $50/month premium hike will significantly increase the number of lower-paid employees who relinquish their insurance coverage because they just can't afford the additional cost. Financial security and affordability are the major issues for our employees in the bottom quarter of the pay scale. For the others it's a mixture of priorities, with no single factor standing out:

- Fairness to those with special conditions by insuring everyone on the same terms
- Job security that comes from a strong and profitable company
- Providing top-quality treatment
- Refusing to balance the financial health of the organization on the backs of the lowest-paid employees."

> *At the constitutional level where we work, 90 percent of any decision is emotional. The rational part of us supplies the reasons for supporting our predilections.*
> **Justice William O. Douglas**

Not only do effective leaders pay attention to values when making decisions, they also reach for the values' deeper meaning. In both public and private settings, skilled decision-makers are deliberate and intentional, comfortable with reason and emotion, analysis, and passion.

Effective leaders identify, understand, and explain their own values. They elicit opinions and listen to what matters to others who have a stake in the decision. They are able and willing to prioritize among a range of competing values, holding on to the most important ones while, perhaps with regret, setting aside others. Finally, they make decisions that flow from what they determine to be most important in each particular situation. The ability to listen to others and understand what matters to them is a critical skill that separates excellent leaders from the run-of-the-mill. They know how to deepen their knowledge.

> *Details are confusing. It is only by selection, by eliminating, by emphasis that we get to the real meaning of things.*
> **Georgia O'Keefe**

Theresa: "I've prepared a list of important values to consider before we weigh our options:

- Fairness to employees with expensive and unusual conditions, since the way we handle this could apply to other cases in the future
- Affordability of the overall plan, so our lower-paid employees can participate
- Financial security of the company by keeping any change cost-neutral to the operating budget
- Maintaining our reputation as a good place to work, so that we can continue to recruit motivated, qualified employees
- Compassion for Mrs. Romero and her unique predicament.

"Let's sleep on this and meet tomorrow morning to see if we can establish what is most important."

## COMPETING GOODS

After moving from gathering and understanding values to weighing them, we begin to test a sense of allegiance or commitment. The most challenging decisions are not about right vs. wrong or good vs. bad. Instead, they are choices between right and right—where we must compromise, neglect, or even violate one important value in order to honor another. Consider some examples of competing values:

- Safety from terrorist attack and privacy from government surveillance both matter.
- Life is precious, as is an individual's right to make private medical decisions, such as refusing treatment to maintain or extend that life.
- Small, locally controlled hospital boards weigh the advantages of remaining independent and responsive to community stakeholders against

a merger with a large out-of-state chain to gain security and increased capability.

- Parents balance the financial benefits of relocating to take a better job with the social disruption such a move might cause their teenage children.

Which value should lead? While additional information rarely dissolves such dilemmas, focused attention and reflection can detect certain gravitational pulls.

> Strategy is a matter of the heart as well as the head. Values and basic beliefs exercise a real gravitational pull on the organization's direction.
>
> **Benjamin Tregoe**

Organizational core values and mission statements offer little guidance in dealing with wrenching choices when more than one option has right and goodness on its side. Ethics audits in business and government usually take a minimalist approach. They ask: *"Have we broken the law?"* and *"Are we in compliance?"* If the answers are *no* and *yes*, discussion of ethics often stops. Yet, it is at this point that the real discussion must begin. It is also where the going gets tricky.

Ask a follow-on question: *"What is our best course of action?"* or *"What matters most to us?"* This shifts the conversation away from a minimalist approach (avoiding what is bad) and puts it on an aspirational path (doing the best we can). It is possible to address inevitable, uncomfortable realities while making a full effort toward an ideal.

Obeying the law, complying with rules and regulations, and avoiding wrongdoing might be costly or inconvenient, but it is usually clear that doing so is in our best interest. Not so obvious is the benefit from turning our backs on important people and values. It hurts to forsake something or someone who matters to us. We do so not because we all win or because we relish someone else's pain. We do so because we see no other choice. Few if any of the difficult choices we confront permit us to honor everything we value. Few if any important decisions benefit everyone and burden no one. Good decisions are forged from competing goods.

In complex or high-stakes decisions, it is especially important that we confront important values that are in tension. By acknowledging that some values must be favored over others, we lay the foundation for a sound decision. Regret is part

> Not everything that counts can be counted. Not everything that can be counted counts.
>
> **Sign in Albert Einstein's office**

of the price to be paid for our thorough analysis and careful attention. When we understand who is involved and what matters to them, we appreciate why some will be disappointed, hurt, or angry.

**The next morning. . .**

Jerry: "I have to tell you, there's something about Ruby Romero's predicament that really gets to me. I'm usually a pretty strong numbers guy, but this is about much more than Mrs. Romero and it goes way beyond numbers. After all, any one of us—or a member of our family—could find ourselves in Mrs. Romero's shoes. If we leave her behind, what message does that send to our employees? So what am I saying is most important? Maybe it's a combination of fairness and compassion . . . there but for the grace of God go I."

John: "I know where I stand. I stand for the greater good. Sure, I'd like to take care of Mrs. Romero *and* our lower-paid employees who live paycheck to paycheck. But if it comes down to a choice, I want to make sure most people in our

> *A great many people think they are thinking when they are merely rearranging their predjudices.*
> **William James**

company can stay insured. The tragedy of one individual's circumstances shouldn't draw our attention away from the critical needs of dozens of other families."

Theresa: "As usual, I can see it both ways. Mrs. Romero and those in similar situations are important, and our lower-paid employees and their families are important. But I've got to consider what best protects the company's financial position over time, so we can continue as a stable, dependable employer. We don't help our employees if we have to lay them off. We haven't talked about options yet, but I expect I'll go with the one that keeps us strong and competitive."

Cognitive dissonance is the tension and discomfort we feel when experiencing irreconcilable ideas or concerns. In order to avoid feeling this tension, it is tempting to rationalize and justify eliminating the conflict in the name of common sense or ethics. *"Anyone can see that what really matters is . . ."* or *"The right thing to do is clear and unambiguous. We just need the courage of our convictions."* In the context of a difficult decision where values conflict, a decision-maker might downplay the impact on a particular value or group. By glossing over the relevance of a particular value, the tension dissolves, the discomfort goes away, and the way forward seems clear.

> *Of the several factors that contribute to wisdom, I should put first a sense of proportion: the capacity to take account of all the important factors in a problem and to attach to each its due weight.*
> **Bertrand Russell**

In our work with various groups, we have noticed ways in which people gloss over discomfort. First, decision-makers can bypass tension by fast-forwarding to a discussion of solutions. Limiting or completely bypassing the values conversation insures that competing goods remain hidden, unacknowledged, and unaddressed. Second, decision-makers may neglect to consider all affected stakeholders, camouflaging competing values and the tension or discomfort they bring. When important values remain unexamined, decisions often unravel.

Finally, there is the well-documented phenomenon of groupthink, a false sense of agreement or approval. Groupthink happens when individuals mold their true opinions to a perceived or imagined group norm. When a supervisor reaches the end of a topic under discussion and asks, *"Does anyone have any other ideas?"* his literal words may invite additional views. The context and tone, however, send the real message: *"No one has anything else to add,* **do you?"**

Sometimes groupthink pressures are subtler than the voice of authority. It is not so much that others silence us as that we silence ourselves. A sense of group cohesion is powerful. Most of us are reluctant to disturb it. The loyalty that each of us feels to family, team, or organization is a powerful value that may outweigh our commitment to honesty. When people don't speak up, decisions suffer. The decision-maker has a key role in making sure everyone has the opportunity to share ideas.

## GUIDING VALUES

In order to settle on a few guiding values, we must work with thoughts infused with feeling. Effective decision-makers know how to tune in to these preferences. For each of us, the cues may be somewhat different. The Quakers speak of the need to listen for a still, small voice within. For others, the sense of what is most important may come from a wordless, intuitive "knowing." While the process may be unique and personal, the task of paying attention and noting our cues is essential.

> *Wisdom is one thing, to know how to make true judgment, how all things are steered through all things.*
> **Heraclitus**

Here, as in step two, reflection and dialogue with others create the space and openness necessary for establishing a hierarchy of guiding values. The goal of this step is to speak to what carries the most weight and then to commit to what will become our guiding values.

Theresa: "After hearing each of you express what is most important, I'm still feeling really torn. Can we take a few more minutes and go over our key points? And this time, I'd like us to reflect back what we hear from one another. That may help me get a feel for what is at the center of this."

**Ten minutes later...**

John: "Jerry, what seems to be most important for you is loyalty to valued employees. We shouldn't leave them behind. Theresa, am I correct that for you it's important that the way to keep our organization financially sound is by keeping our valued employees? You both seem to focus on the importance of supporting individual employees, although for somewhat different reasons." (Both nod) "I continue to see it differently. You have given my concerns a fair hearing, and I don't sense that more discussion will help us bridge our different priorities. Theresa, when you report to Jane, please explain my position clearly. If there is a way to help the lowest-paid employees deal with the cost increase

## Finding the Guiding Values

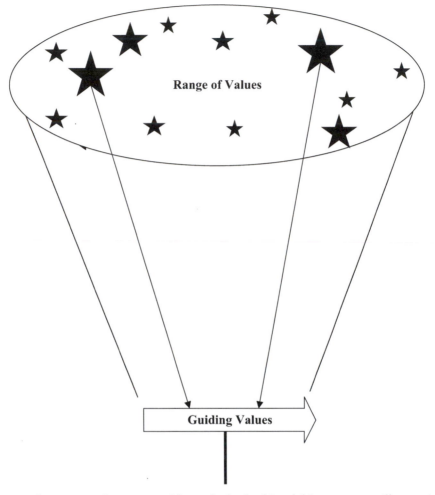

so they can regain coverage, I hope the leadership of this company will commit to make it happen."

Often, consensus is not possible. Conscientious dialogue and reflection may leave a management team or a family with clear, irreconcilable differences. However, there is something powerful and positive that remains after genuine dialogue where everyone has been given a fair hearing. Respectful disagreement usually leaves relationships intact and lays the foundation for openness and meaningful exchange in the future. Acrimonious debate often ends with people feeling disregarded, marginalized, and angry. Such disagreement leads naturally to ruptured relationships, attempts to sabotage the decision, and future conflicts.

**Afterwards, Theresa reports to Jane**

Theresa: "Jerry, John, and I have carefully reviewed the situation. We could not reach a consensus recommendation. After weighing all the options, Jerry and I decided that the best course of action is to let Geneco raise the premium amount while keeping the current coverage intact. Although Mrs. Romero's situation is compelling in itself, we based our recommendation on a fundamental sense of fairness to all employees and members of their families who now or in the future may develop an expensive or rare condition.

We recognize that a likely consequence of this decision will be that some of our lower-paid employees will drop coverage because they can't afford the added cost. Unfortunately, our current budget doesn't allow for the company to pick up the increase for them. So, in the short term, some of our employees and their families may not be able to afford coverage. We have no solution to this negative impact. John advocated strongly that the needs of the many outweighed the dramatic but limited needs of Mrs. Romero. He recommends that the administration make this personnel cost item a priority and attempt to find a solution in the next fiscal year."

## WHAT YOU CAN DO

### *Separate Commitment from Options*

The goal: Establish a firm foundation for the decision by restating and confirming the principles before turning to available options.

Many of us are instinctive problem solvers. We scan a situation, listen to others briefly, and immediately begin to consider what to do. While this tendency can serve us well in some situations, prematurely shifting the focus to the outcome can limit essential understanding of important values. When this happens, you miss an important opportunity to increase clarity and conviction.

### Capture Solutions but Defer Discussion of Options

It is important to encourage ideas and remain mindful of how easy it is to squelch creative, resourceful insights. When ideas and proposals come forward, acknowledge them and write them down. If you are working with a group, assure the person proposing a solution that his idea will be taken up later. *"I can see you're ready to decide what to do. Can we just make a note of your suggestion and come back to it in a minute? I still need to understand what is most important to you before deciding how to proceed."*

*"Why not write your idea down on the board? That way we won't lose it and we can spend more time hearing about what we each feel is at the heart of this."*

### Go Deeper into Values Instead of Jumping to Options

The values content of an issue can be like an iceberg. To reveal what is below the visible surface, slow down and go beneath early statements of important values. *"John, you have come back to fairness in health insurance several times, but I still don't understand what that word means to you. Are you using it in a couple of different ways?"*

### Organize the Values List

In order to keep the focus on what matters most, a visual reference helps. Make sure to summarize the discussion with some kind of list or outline. It may be helpful to group or sort the key values in one of a variety of ways. Take fifteen to thirty minutes to organize and tighten the list before moving to any ranking. *"As we look at this list, what can we do to make it more useful? Could we group the values into categories?"*

More work may be needed before participants can compare values. For example, some words, like "integrity," are too big to stand alone. Define and connect such values words to the context at hand. *"For me, integrity means keeping commitments previously made."* In addition, some elements of a large concept like integrity may conflict with one another. For example, we may commit to protect someone's privacy (keeping commitments made), yet we may also believe it's important to reveal a source of information (being honest and open) to protect our credibility. *"Are all of these words clear, or do we need to say more about what each of us means?"*   .

### If You Are on Your Own. . .

Ask yourself if you are clear and committed to one to three key values. What are they? Break the big words down into practical statements about what is really important to you. Then write them down. The act of putting your thoughts and feelings on paper is even more important when you are alone. Other people are mirrors who reflect back to you what you express as significant. Without them, you need to find a way to look back at yourself and your values.

### *Encourage Transparent Advocacy*

The goal: Develop a clear sense of priorities and the reasoning that supports their priority.

When you address what you care about deeply and passionately, there is an element of advocacy, even when you do not intend to persuade someone else. Make space for everyone's heartfelt discourse. When everyone has the same opportunity, the process remains open and fair, and you come to understand others better.

### Make Room for Advocacy

Call for an advocacy round in which all participants identify their top values and briefly describe the reasons for their choices. *"Let's take time to focus on the key values we think must be reflected in a final decision. I want each of you to identify one value that you believe is critical in this situation and explain why.*"

You can compress or expand the time this takes to fit the constraints of the situation. In fifteen minutes or less, each member of a six-person team could take two minutes to identify the most important values and why they were chosen. With less time, ask for only one choice and the reason. Encourage participants to keep their reasoning brief. If you have thirty to forty-five minutes, follow the advocacy round with discussion and clarification to deepen the understanding of the choice. *"Now that everyone has weighed in once, what should we come back to and dig a bit deeper?"*

### Take a Vote

It takes about five minutes to follow the advocacy round with multiple voting. This simple technique allows each participant three to five votes. Make sure the values are listed in front of everyone. Put a mark or sticky note next to an item. Tally the votes, and place the items in a shorter list with the most votes at the top. With limited time, this becomes the final list to use in the search for a solution. If time permits, it can be useful to take at least ten to twenty minutes to discuss participants' responses to the results. These responses may include concerns, observations, or questions.

Consider having participants commit to their votes privately by writing them down before they see what others do. Students of group dynamics observe that this step increases the likelihood of obtaining participants' honest opinions and avoids undue influence by other group members. Another way to insure that each person gives an honest opinion is to note his vote on a piece of paper. Gather these ballots and tally the results for all to see.

A variation of multiple voting is weighted multiple voting. If each participant has five votes, he can apportion them to one or more items reflecting his sense of relative importance. For example, an item that is much more important to an individual than all others might receive four votes with another item receiving one vote.

In some situations, a comprehensive ranking of all the items on the list is productive. Thus, with a list of ten values, each is ranked from one to ten, where ten is the most important. Add all participants' rankings for each item and divide the total by the number of participants to come up with an average for each item.

If you list the values on a flip chart or white board, mark each item on the list with a star or dot of a different color each time a participant mentions it in the advocacy round. This creates a visual record of emerging patterns of priority and emphasis.

### Look at Values Side by Side

It may be difficult to prioritize a long or complex list of values. Try using the technique of paired-comparison analysis, which compares items, two at a time, in isolation from the rest. "*When you think about compassion for our lowest-paid employees and their families and weigh that against the importance of keeping a health plan that covers rare and expensive conditions, which is more important to our company at this time?*"

By narrowing the focus, we can sharpen the distinctions among the most important values.

See the "Pair Analysis" worksheet in the Appendix.

### If You are on Your Own. . .

Without others to advocate for key values, keep the values in front of you to allow enough time and reflection to consider priority among them. Side-by-side comparison is the easiest way to do this.

### *Explore Differences*

The goal: Deepen the dialogue as you approach the heart of the matter.

To encourage honesty and respect in our relationships at work, in the community, and in our families, we have to make it emotionally safe to disagree and differ. Instead of pulling back when we sense the tension of actual or perceived differences, we must move toward differences with curiosity and the intent to learn more. This behavior sends an affirming message. While the differences have not evaporated, we acknowledge them openly. It also becomes easier to remember what we have in common. Instead of polarizing separation, we find connection.

### Change Shoes

As the process moves toward what is most important, it is easy for participants to become more intense and emotional in expressing themselves. Don't let the dialogue slip into debate where participants criticize others or score points. "*I have the sense that we have stopped listening before responding to each other. Ted, would you be willing to go over your concerns again? I'd like everyone to give Ted a fair hearing before responding.*"

Another challenging way to shift the dynamics and encourage a more productive exchange is to ask people on opposing sides to try to represent the other side's point of view, as sincerely as possible. "*If we traded positions for a few minutes, it might help us understand our differences. Ed, how would you put my concerns in the most favorable light possible?*"

## Speak about Uncertainty and Wonder

The closer you get to principles and issues that matter to you, the easier it is to fall into the trap of passionate certainty. Conviction is good. But global or sweeping statements of moral certitude often shut others down, polarize the communication, and encourage debate instead of dialogue. When you can speak passionately while acknowledging doubt and uncertainty, some space stays in the exchange so others can also acknowledge their doubts. *"I know that I want to take care of Mrs. Romero, but what I don't know is where that principle takes us in other, similar cases. Health care costs and technological innovation will only lead us to greater and greater expense. We have to set boundaries on what a health plan covers. There has to be a limit. When will we get there?"*

It is hard to confess doubt. One way to admit uncertainty is to wonder. *"I am trying to imagine what will happen with the lower-paid employees if premiums go up* and *we tell them that employer coverage of the increase will be considered after this tough fiscal year ends."* This kind of thinking aloud can move you out of the box, engage values, and acknowledge uncertainty, albeit indirectly.

## Use the Power of Silence

For some, the power of wisdom comes only when they tap their intuitive, feeling-based thoughts. For this to happen, they need space by themselves— in the room, at the conference table, or in the conversation. Youth soccer players who naturally converge on the ball at all times learn that in order to become more skillful with passing and ball movement, they must run to space. Only by moving away from the ball (running to space on the field) do they create opportunities to interact with the ball in different and successful ways. If values are the ball, you may need to use silence to get away from the constant focus on values and create an opportunity to move the discussion forward. *"Could we take a break and clear our heads for a few minutes? It gets pretty heated when we talk about the core of this issue."*

Avoid groupthink. Make sure that before advocacy occurs, participants have the opportunity to reflect privately and develop their own considered views of the key, guiding values. Continue your core practice of reflective listening to insure that participants hear and feel heard. *"I'd like each of us to write down our preferences and commit to them before hearing from anyone else. Although it is OK to be persuaded by what someone else says, I want each of us to share what he or she wrote down as most important and why."*

## If You are on Your Own. . .

It is challenging to try to see as others see, but it can be done. You can change shoes without the help of others. However, it is easy to underestimate the passion that others will bring to this issue. Ask yourself, *"Am I fairly considering their point of view on this issue?"*

Find the kind of quiet, reflective space you know works best for you, in order to access your wisest self. Consider going for a walk, sitting in meditation, writing about the situation in a journal, or taking a shower.

**Remember:**

- Be clear about the few, bright guiding values that point you toward the final decision.
- More important than agreement is a sense by all participants that each has had the opportunity to advocate for the values he believes are most significant.
- Most important is a sense by everyone that each has been heard and understood.

See the "Worksheet for Step 3: Commit to What Matters Most" in the Appendix.

**Consider another difficult decision at work. . .**

A dedicated employee of a social service agency feels caught between the requirements of her job and the needs of a friend. As you read the story, ask yourself the following questions.

- Which way do you lean in this situation?
- How would you describe the competing goods in this right vs. right decision?
- If you were to explain to someone what, for you, is the heart of the matter, what would you say? Why?

Diane Gomez is the director of an outreach program at an inner city agency whose mission is job training for poor women. She spoke with her boss this morning, and the news is bad. The program she has led for fifteen years is going to end in sixty days, due to funding cutbacks. Last-ditch efforts to secure replacement grants and new funding have failed. All the employees Diane has trained and supervised over the years will lose their jobs.

Diane is close to her employees and thinks of several of them as family. Many of her employees started as clients of the agency—single mothers struggling to climb out of poverty. Diane has been both mentor and friend to those women as they faced challenges such as abusive relationships, substance and alcohol use, and children caught up in gangs.

When Diane indicated she wanted to inform her staff about the layoffs, her boss explained that the agency was following the advice of an outside human resources consultant to delay the announcement until the last possible moment.

"Three years ago, we had to drop a program and lay off five people. We gave ninety days notice, and it was a disaster. Our computers were sabotaged and productivity went to zero. Staff will not be told for another thirty days. We don't want to affect morale any sooner than necessary. Nor do we want to place ourselves at risk for any kind of sabotage."

Diane went to bat for her employees, insisting that it was only fair to inform them as soon as possible. Many of her employees are single parents who live paycheck to paycheck. Without sufficient time to deal with the layoff, they will be unable to find other work. The financial blow could be devastating for them and their families. Her boss responded by directing Diane to keep the layoff confidential for another month and declaring the discussion closed.

Two days later, a veteran employee of the program and friend came to Diane and asked if she knew anything about a rumor floating around that their program was ending. When Diane hesitated, the coworker became upset and said, "I'm in a jam, and I've got to know if there's any truth to this. I found a house to buy, and I am making an offer this week. The down payment will take all my savings, and with my paycheck, I can barely cover the mortgage. If I'm going to be out of a job soon, I don't want to get in over my head. **Do you know anything?**"

# 4

---

# Choose to Act

---

*It is not what a lawyer tells me that I may do; but what humanity,
reason, and justice tell me I ought to do.*

                                                    **Edmund Burke**

Somewhere along the road to a decision, we come to a crossroads. The
gathering, reviewing, and analyzing phase is behind us. The options lie
before us, and the time has come to choose our direction—to walk the talk.

Decisions come in all sizes and categories. When we perceive the decision
as minor, the road toward it is short, straight, and one we are likely to travel
in private. But sometimes we find ourselves on a crowded super highway,
facing a high-profile decision whose every aspect will be magnified—and
judged—by very public scrutiny.

## MEDICINE, MISSION, AND MORAL FITNESS

Bethany Memorial is a nondenominational, nonprofit hospital with 400 beds.
Located in Capital City, a major metropolitan area, it maintains a strong relationship with the state's only medical school. Because of its size, location, and prominence in the health care field, it receives extensive media coverage for policy
issues, particularly if they involve controversy.

Enter Dr. John William Seraphy. Some time ago he submitted an application for
medical staff privileges at Bethany Memorial. Although the medical executive committee conducted exhaustive initial and follow-up interviews with Dr. Seraphy, his
application has been held longer than any review in the hospital's history. Now, the
committee is deadlocked, and the hospital's CEO has named a community advisory
board composed of prominent citizens to make an independent recommendation.

Twenty years ago, at the age of sixteen, John Seraphy was convicted of murdering Bradley Fitch, also a physician here in Capital City. Dr. Fitch had been a longtime friend of the Seraphy family—so close he was always referred to as "Uncle" Brad by young Seraphy. Following the trial, Seraphy was sentenced to life imprisonment, the harshest sentence possible for a juvenile. Intense media coverage of the brutal homicide included details of "mutilation," emphasizing that the young perpetrator exhibited "remarkable coldness" and showed "no remorse." At the time, Seraphy's own comments and testimony raised questions that he might be psychotic.

Several years later, new details of the case emerged, including credible evidence that, as a boy, Seraphy had been chronically and cruelly abused by Dr. Fitch, both emotionally and sexually. (Seraphy's parents, whose testimony at the trial registered shock and surprise at the deed, were later killed in an auto accident; if they suspected their friend's transgressions, their misgivings were buried with them.) This new information, taken with Seraphy's exemplary behavior in prison, including graduation from high school and college, prompted a prominent human rights activist to organize a

> *Let no one say that taking action is hard. Action is aided by courage, by the moment, by impulse, and the hardest thing in the world is making a deceision.*
> **Franz Grillparzer**

campaign to free him. Twelve years ago, Governor Jones commuted his sentence to time already served, and Seraphy was released. Some time later, Governor Smith issued a full pardon, restoring all Dr. Seraphy's legal rights. The governor based the pardon on extraordinary achievement (graduation from medical school with highest honors) and dedicated service to the community (five years of work as the medical director of an inner-city clinic in Chicago).

Other area hospitals in Capital City have already granted Dr. Seraphy temporary privileges without controversy. When Dr. Seraphy's application to Bethany Memorial became public, the state's largest newspaper began editorializing in favor of his acceptance. The editorials not only raised questions about the delays in his application review but also sharply questioned the integrity of the hospital and further challenged Bethany to live up to its declared core value of compassion.

Dr. Seraphy's academic and medical training clearly exceeds the standards usually applied to physicians seeking privileges at Bethany Memorial. His application was thoroughly verified. All responses and references are superlative. He has never had a lawsuit filed against him. His area of practice is currently underrepresented on the hospital staff, so he would be a valuable addition from a skills perspective. Still, many current members of the hospital staff remember the murder; were friends, colleagues, or acquaintances of the late Dr. Fitch; and have never forgotten the brutal details of the case.

The fourth challenge is to walk our talk, that is, to put our values into practice. To walk one's talk implies that actions align with statements of belief about what is important. In a sense, each significant decision is a pop quiz that tests us on our values.

There is no shortage of commentary about the gap between the talk and the walk. Media commentators portray themselves as ethics experts and freely scold their audience about the erosion of morality and character in public and private life. More than a few have been exposed as hypocrites when their own conduct fell short of the standards they demanded of others.

> When you have a choice and don't make it, that is, in itself, a choice.
>
> **William James**

As we have already noted, defining choices often come upon us suddenly. The choice may necessarily involve others, or we may truly be alone in our deliberations. When we endeavor to choose based on our understanding of what is most important, we accomplish two things. First, we pass the "sleep test"; that is, we sleep with a clear conscience regarding our sense of integrity. Second, we lay the groundwork for meeting the final challenge—communicating to others the real basis for our decision.

This chapter explores three dimensions of choosing wisely. First, we must understand what **choice** is and how it works. Second, choice implies a sense of ownership and attendant responsibility. Our choices reveal who we are and what we stand for. Choice is about **character**. Third, to make choices with our eyes open, aware of the situation and mindful of those involved, we must anticipate and accept responsibility for repercussions, even if we do not wish or intend them. This requires careful consideration of **consequences**.

## THE NATURE OF CHOICE

So far, we have talked about decision and choice without carefully distinguishing between them. The Latin root of decide is *decaedere,* meaning to cut off, cut the knot, determine. A decision results from the overall process of weighing and deliberating in order to make up one's mind. However, this aggressive dimension of deciding by "cutting off" can compromise the integrity of a decision by failing to link the decision with our important values.

Choice implies that we move toward or embrace something because of preference or affinity. A decision propelled by our guiding values is obviously superior to one whose outcome is simply the last option standing. When the focus stays on what matters most, important principles illuminate the consideration of options. Our task, then, is not to rule out options until only one remains but to see how our guiding values pull us toward actions that fit. When we choose, we embrace the action taken. We say, "Yes, I do," instead of holding our nose and saying, "Okay. Whatever." The focus shifts from settling for the lesser of evils to choosing the greater among goods.

The root dynamic of affirmation instead of negation makes a difference. It is a form of decision alchemy that invisibly but powerfully binds the decision-maker to her choice. Because she owns the outcome, the decision-maker becomes more confident about the integrity of her choice. The coherence and the resonance between the guiding values and the choice also increase the likelihood that others will see and

> *I leave this rule for others when I'm dead. Be always sure you're right, then go ahead.*
> **David Crockett**

accept the integrity of the outcome. The credibility of the person or group that owns the decision is clear to those hearing about it.

Current technology complicates choosing. Thanks to the virtual worlds and information galaxies opened up by the Internet, we can go anywhere and find anything. Spreadsheet software and decision tools make it possible to pump out multiple alternatives, scenarios, and variables. Access to more and more and the ability to manipulate again and again are mixed blessings.

In spite of all the noise from information and conflict, sometimes we just know. We may come to an issue with an intuition of what is most important, and we may stay with it throughout the decision-making process. This does not necessarily indicate prejudgment or a closed mind. Even when our guiding star appears early on, the steps up to and until the act of choice help us test this knowing. They deepen our confidence that it is genuine and not illusory.

More often, what matters most to us lies buried in a mound of undifferentiated or disorderly values. The value that first attracts us may not be the one we hold onto. We need time, talk, and reflection to find the right focus. Different views can provide such a reflective medium.

Conversation also helps us find us find an effective way to explain values to others, once we make a decision. When a decision-maker lays off 200 people, disconnects a life-support system, sells the family home, or rejects a permit for a homeless shelter, *"It just seemed like the right thing to do"* is insufficient. Those who bear the burden deserve something more than, *"My gut told me."* It is the clarity, coherence, and power of our driving values that give decisions their integrity. We need to know our own values, capture them in words, and explain them generously and honestly.

For example, the moral quality of a decision to turn off a ventilator depends almost entirely on how the decision-maker reached that decision. Who was (or should have been) involved? What mattered to them? Whose decision was it? And so on. Compare the following two accounts where the final decision is the same. Ask yourself, how do the reasons given contribute to the decision's integrity? Think not so much of a right/wrong dichotomy but more of a graduated scale of integrity. On a scale of one to ten, with ten being the highest degree of integrity possible, how would you grade the following two decisions?

*"My husband and I talked about this before he became sick. We agreed: if either of us is permanently comatose, not able to speak, and the doctors agree that recovery is virtually impossible, then it's time to stop all life-support treatment. That time has come, so please, turn off the ventilator."*

*"This patient is a homeless man, and an alcoholic to boot. We don't have the time or the legal obligation to investigate what he would want done. He may or may not recover, but we just can't continue to waste resources on him. Turn off the ventilator."*

Our approach in this book is to resist the urge to leap to solutions. When participants lock in on the preferred choice too early, there is a natural tendency to spend the remaining time coming up with reasons and arguments to support that conclusion. At best, the premature focus on solutions reduces the values discussion to a sideshow. At worst, it undermines the integrity of the decision by shifting the emphasis to ways to package and "sell" the outcome to stakeholders.

It is natural for participants to come up with possible solutions right from the beginning. Instead, we recommend a more deliberate process that defers extensive identification and generation of options. Participants need to spend time with the values and settle on what is most important before testing possible solutions.

"I can't see that we have a choice. Granted, Dr. Seraphy's successes and contributions are remarkable, but we can't let concerns for one man's mission to heal his past override the morale of an entire hospital. We need to reject his application, take the heat, and move on. I do think, however, we should spend some time considering how to sell this to the public."

When we make a conscious commitment to put important values first, this tell-what-will-sell tendency is less likely to operate. However, it takes real discipline to defer the discussion of ideas, options, or possibilities until a clear understanding develops about what is most important.

> *Our actions are the ground on which we stand.*
> **Gautama Buddha**

When we are clear about our top values, the next task is to generate and examine possible options that honor these values.

"I think we have narrowed this down to three key principles that should guide our action: morale of hospital staff, fairness and consistency in applying hospital standards for medical privileges, and our sense of integrity concerning our health care mission. First, let's lay out the obvious options and then consider whether there are others."

"Why is it either/or? I certainly understand that we can reject his application or recommend that it be accepted. Why can't we also accept it with certain conditions or reject it but agree to reconsider in six to twelve months if certain things happen, such as . . . ."

"Listening to all of you, I see four options:

1. Approve the application with full privileges as requested.
2. Deny the application based upon some or all of the identified concerns.
3. Approve the application with conditions such as:
   a. satisfactory independent psychiatric assessment, or
   b. applicant and concerned staff meeting, with the assistance of a mediator, to determine if a constructive working relationship is possible.
4. Reject the application with some language that permits or encourages Dr. Seraphy to apply again in six months to twelve months if certain conditions are met."

## CHARACTER AND CHOICE

Difficult choices test us. They cost us something. It takes personal courage to face such choices head-on and follow our convictions about what is important.

To repeat, when time permits we should be creative and resourceful in developing a range of options to consider. In some situations, this effort leads to a solution that honors all or most of the important values surrounding a decision. But what if time doesn't permit? What if exhaustive effort and careful analysis leave crucial values in conflict? Subject to time constraints, we must test each available option for fit with our guiding values. How well does it honor or uphold each one? Is there a clear-cut connection between the stated value and the proposed action? Even if others dislike or disagree with the chosen option, will they be able to sense the coherence between the talk and the walk?

> *Many complain about their memory, few about their judgment.*
> **La Rochefoucauld**

"We have a set of core values—do they dictate that we must approve Dr. Seraphy's application? If we don't grant Dr. Seraphy medical privileges, there will surely be an editorial and letters to the editor that question the sincerity of our commitment. However, our mission and our reputation rest on the quality of the service and care we provide to our patients. If our decision honors those values, then I feel our integrity remains intact, no matter what happens in the newspaper."

We use the term character to acknowledge moral strength, the courage to act on our convictions. Whether or not you agree with all his positions, most of us remember Pope John Paul II for his courage to articulate and maintain principled positions, regardless of public opinion. Let's look more carefully at moral values, character as moral strength, and their combined role in decision-making.

Moral values are values we invoke to name what is right and wrong, good and bad in human conduct and character. Most, if not all voters, regardless of political persuasion, hold dear their own set of moral values. The issue is not that some care more about moral values than others do. The problem is agreeing and knowing how to manage conflicts among moral values, not just with others but also within ourselves.

In recent years, some writers and philosophers have focused on the role of virtues—honesty and trustworthiness, for example—as hallmarks of a person's strong moral character. The assumption is that people exhibiting these virtues will behave ethically.

Similarly, businesses hang framed statements of their missions and core values on the walls of conference rooms. Usually, this is an aspirational practice, hopeful that staff struggling with difficult choices will pay attention to these principles. Character education and corporate wall hangings, however, collide with the contemporary, minimalist culture of decision-making.

> *A man's character is formed by his decisions.*
> **Jean Paul Sartre**

Whether it's state and federal government, corporate America, or local community businesses, the decision-making goal frequently drops to the level of simply avoiding breaking the law or violating rules. Understanding ethics as nothing more than avoiding wrongdoing distorts the meaning of moral values and character. There is more to ethical behavior than mere compliance.

Clearly, we should pay attention to moral values and behave according to principles that matter most. Merely exhorting people to be virtuous, however, is not enough. Often these appeals start and stop with compelling but abstract language. For example, we might agree, "*We should be fair.*" What does fairness mean in this situation? When you can't be fair to everyone, who has priority? On what basis do you prioritize?

> *In matters of style, swim with the current. In matters of principle, stand like a rock.*
> **Thomas Jefferson**

Where does your standard of fairness come from? To bring moral principles to life, we must talk about them in specific situations where their meaning comes alive. You and I may refer to the same moral value but understand and apply it very differently.

"I have to say it bothers me when you talk about fairness for Dr. Seraphy. This clearly isn't just about his credentials, as it is with 99.9 percent of all the other applicants. This man murdered his parents' lifelong friend—a man who was also both friend and colleague of some of our employees! It's as though we're asking people who were traumatized to overlook that—or worse, that we are requiring them to forgive him. I don't think forgiveness works like that, and I don't want to sacrifice the morale of our hospital on the altar of forgiveness. This is not a case of staff refusal to accept a physician because he is Asian, black, or Muslim. This is not about an all-male surgical staff being uncomfortable with the first woman surgeon. That would be unfair, and our decision would be crystal clear. This is different."

Important principles flourish when we engage with others to build and sharpen their meaning. How can we bring our values alive in conversation? How can we apply them in a specific situation with real people, history, and human relationships? How can we avoid slipping into moral relativism where anything goes, where fairness leads us in one direction today but in another tomorrow? Motivational speakers and character programs offer scant guidance about how to make a choice that is accountable, both for the values it honors as well as those it must leave behind.

Our values are our guiding stars. Often it is through reflection and dialogue with others that we come to see how our values work in a given situation and where they lead us. This takes strength and resolve. It requires courage. Courage may require physical strength or endurance. It may conjure up the image of a solitary individual wrestling with an agonizing dilemma. Most of our difficult choices, however, arrive as packages wrapped in relationships and interdependence. The strength required is psychological because the courage we describe is the willingness to listen well to others and open ourselves to the possibility that we might be changed by what they say.

> *Courage is the first among human qualities because it is the one on which all others depend.*
> **Aristotle**

"You're right, this **is** different. I believe we have to consider the impact on teamwork and morale, because the quality of our patient care is the heart of who we are. What troubles me is giving up, which is how I interpret rejecting the application out of hand. I know we can't mandate forgiveness, but could we take steps to give it a chance to appear? Are we willing to face this directly instead of just making it go away?"

## CHOICE AND CONSEQUENCES

Finally, there is the aspect of choice that none of us enjoys looking at directly: the fact that no choice is entirely satisfactory. Someone will bear the burden; we will compromise or set aside some value(s). It is only natural to

## Guiding Values at the Crossroads

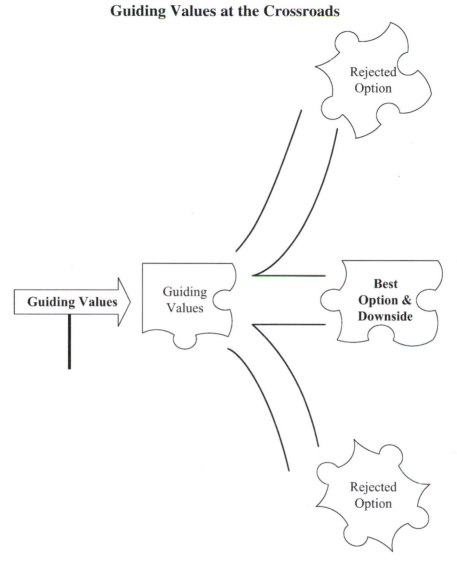

want a win-win situation, where everyone involved winds up satisfied. We resist the harsh reality that a difficult choice is not pain-free. In order to

> *Wisdom consists of the anticipation of consequences.*
> **Norman Cousins**

uphold what is most important, we must set aside something that is also important. When we move forward, we leave something behind. To choose one good, we let another one go. A good decision includes the price paid. Effective decision-makers do not conceal the cost.

There are two common downsides in most tough choices. First, there are negative consequences for some stakeholders. Before we settle on the best option, we need to consider how it will affect people and their values. Whom will this option burden or hurt? We must be concrete and brutally honest. A decision that doesn't look at this is a setup for outrage and resistance from

> *Nothing pains some people more than having to think.*
> **Martin Luther King Jr.**

people who believe their concerns were not considered. No matter how good the decision looks to us, to others, the emperor has no clothes. By failing to consider harm to others, we place our own credibility at risk. As others see us, either we are incompetent for failing to consider likely consequences or callous and indifferent to the effect on others.

Second, there are regrets. Regrets include consequences, but a decision-maker can also regret not being able to include an important value in the decision. If other values such as safety or product quality also matter but do not appear in the decision, how should we deal with their lesser status? Excluded values create uncomfortable feelings of dissonance.

While it is easy to deny or overlook unintended consequences, good decisions can unravel from such inattention. To protect the quality of a decision, think twice about results that you don't desire or intend (but that could possibly occur). Try differentiating between what might happen and what almost certainly will happen. Consider assessing the consequences and categorizing them as follows:

- What is likely to happen? (>75 percent chance)
- What will probably happen? (50–75 percent chance)
- What may possibly happen? (25–50 percent chance)
- What is unlikely but could happen? (<25 percent chance).

This kind of analysis helps us avoid a common error in decision-making—overconfidence. When we consider only what we want to have happen and underestimate or ignore the possibility of unfavorable outcomes, we are apt to be blind-sided by events once we act on our decision. Instead of wishing away or ignoring the negatives, we should ac-

> *Both faith and cynicism make judgment too easy.*
> **Mason Cooley**

knowledge them. We should test our decision for possible consequences. By doing so we increase the likelihood that the benefits will outweigh the costs. It also gives us insight and information necessary for our fifth and final challenge, communicating the decision honestly and transparently.

A colleague of ours works as an ombudsman in a large technical organization. He observes that his highly educated colleagues frequently argue that they should be held accountable only for their intentions, not the actual consequences of their decisions. That a class of highly trained workers, many with advanced degrees in engineering and science, should hold such a view suggests how hard it is to confront what causes us discomfort.

A risk to this approach is that we simply react to and recoil from predictions of bad consequences. By choosing and affirming what matters most (not merely moving away from the worst) and by committing to an honest appraisal of foreseeable consequences, we can evaluate them and assign them an appropriate place in a decision. They are neither missing in action nor so overwhelming that they paralyze.

> *A good decision is based on knowledge and not on numbers.*
> **Plato**

We are not talking about perfection or all-seeing wisdom. There is a relatively simple way to deal productively with consequences. As you settle upon the option that most naturally connects to your guiding values, look down the road ahead. Consider how others will review your decision. What are its possible and probable consequences?

"What do we think might happen as a result of our decision? What will be the impacts on Bethany Memorial's staff if we approve Dr. Seraphy's application? In returning to the scene of the crime as it were, Dr. Seraphy would be interacting with employees who knew and worked with his victim, and where a number of people have vivid memories of the crime. At least five members of the medical staff have made it clear that they will not work with him. Two of our most experienced nurses were devoted to Dr. Fitch and happen to be eligible for retirement. They have written letters stating that they will retire rather than work with him. Due to the nursing shortage, their experience and skills are irreplaceable."

"If Seraphy's application is rejected because of staff concerns and statements about resigning, what message does this send to staff about their power to shape policy through threats?"

"I see your point, but how likely is it that any significant number of staff will conclude that threats work, given the extreme circumstances in this case?"

"Because of the sensational details of the crime and its impact on potential patients who might be alarmed and/or mistrustful, this will not be a quiet hire. There will be intense media coverage. What if this mistrust attaches to Bethany Memorial? On the other hand, negative publicity about the hospital's mission and treatment of Dr. Seraphy may also impact the public's image of the institution."

> *Two roads diverged in a wood, and I—I took the one less traveled by, and that has made all the difference.*
> **Robert Frost**

"Is there an issue of safety here? I'm not just talking about our personnel and our patients but Dr. Seraphy himself. There's always the possibility—however remote—that someone out there will turn violent and try to exact retribution. I hate to bring this up, but it happens."

"There is also concern about the applicant's rehabilitation. Is it genuine? There is no definitive psychological or psychiatric evaluation available. The applicant describes himself as self-rehabilitated through reading spiritual books, personal reflection during his time in prison, and transformation furthered by serving an inner-city clinic in Chicago. Does he have a mental illness that has never been satisfactorily addressed? When asked if he would meet directly with those physicians

> *To have a right to do a thing is not at all the same as being right in doing it.*
> G. K. Chesterton

and nurses apprehensive about working with him, Seraphy shook his head and said, 'I'm sorry, but I've worked very hard to put all that behind me. I think my record as a physician speaks for itself. My hope is that they will come to accept me for who I am now. If they can't, well, I'm sorry.' When asked if he had any psychiatric/psychological assessment information, Seraphy indicated he did not. When asked if he would submit to an independent examination, he stated that he would not."

## WHAT YOU CAN DO

### Expand the Possibilities

The goal: Develop and explore the range of options available.

This effort usually starts with ideas participants have already identified. Even with a short deadline, a little time and attention can produce additional alternatives, even if they are only variations on existing ideas.

### Take a Step Back

If possible, allow time and space to pursue more ideas. That's not easy when you live in a "hurry-up" mode. In the interest of closure, creativity goes out the window and the decision-maker overlooks important options. When a tough decision looms, there is a tendency to latch on to one of the obvious options instead of taking the time to develop others. Much can be accomplished with a little more time. Still, try adjourning the meeting and doing some homework to determine whether a particular option is available. Consult stakeholders. Investigate key information.

*"Have any other hospitals faced a similar question involving a doctor with a criminal record as a minor? If so, how did they handle it? Harry, will you call the general counsel at the State Hospital Association and ask about her familiarity with related situations?"*

*"I question our need to decide today. We have a tentative decision. Let's take the weekend to let it sit and meet again on Monday morning. If no one has come up with a better possibility to consider, we're done."*

## See the Perfect as the Enemy of the Good

Sometimes, it is difficult or impossible to see down the road. Perhaps a viable option is not available at this time. In situations like this, consider taking modest next steps that move the decision process forward while keeping final options open. At the same time, make an effort to develop additional options that better reflect important values. It may be that an interim or more limited decision will provide enough time to make a more thoughtful choice. Remember the proverb: *"If you don't have time to do it right, when do you have time to do it over?"*

*"I know the press may put some heat on as long as this application is pending. But why not recommend taking another week to bring in an independent mental health expert. She could review the original murder case file, the pardon file about the abuse evidence, and assess the possibility of an undiagnosed, untreated condition that might affect Dr. Seraphy's fitness to practice medicine."*

## Stretch Your Creative Muscles

Encourage the participants to be creative in developing options. This effort doesn't need to be wild-eyed or impractical. It is about taking a little time, having an open attitude, and refraining from immediate comments and critical judgments that shut down the flow of ideas. Here are three ways to increase the number of possibilities under consideration.

Ask the open question, *"What if . . . ?"*

*"What if we ask the hospital chaplain to facilitate an informal meeting between Dr. Seraphy and four of his most vocal opponents?"*

*"What if we considered a grant of temporary privileges to Dr. Seraphy for thirty days to see how his presence affects hospital operations? The privileges would automatically sunset unless the committee formally approved them at the end of the trial period."*

Create more options to test against the driving values by combining different elements of existing ideas. Add or take away something from an existing option. For example, change the scope of a decision by changing a permanent policy decision to a six-month trial period.

*"Are there different parts of these three options that we could mix and match to come up with another option?"*

Reverse the way you are looking at the situation by changing your perspective. For example, consider an organization that has to make a public statement about a mistake that could put it in a bad light. Instead of looking at what to do from the point of view of damage control, what options emerge if it is viewed as a unique opportunity to build or rebuild public trust?

*"What if we stopped looking at this like a community advisory board and started looking at this like a patient who doesn't know anything about the way the hospital operates? Does that suggest a way to respond?"*

### If You Are on Your Own. . .

You can apply all of these ideas directly. It may help if you keep a white board or pad of paper handy so you can write down ideas as soon as they occur to you.

### *Find the Fit*

The goal: Reach a clear decision that directly links to the most important values.

The connection between a guiding value and a choice speaks more loudly than words. Everything up to this point lays the groundwork for the decisive moment. This is the source of authentic power and integrity. Fight the urge to gloss over this critical work. If the connection isn't clear to you, how can it be clear to those who will hear about your decision?

### Use a Tuning Fork

Piano tuners use a piece of metal that vibrates to sound a note that can be matched to the sound of a key. There is an emotional tuning fork you can sound to help match options with your guiding values. There are different ways to use this capacity. Try speaking the values that are important to you along with the following words: *"And because [your guiding values] matter so much to me, I have decided to [state the option]."*

Pause after each statement and feel the sound of it. Does it resonate? Do you notice any dissonance? Do any of the statements have a particular rightness or wrongness that registers as you speak them? Remember, this is about how it feels to you, not what you think.

*"When I imagine telling the CEO about my recommendation, I just get this sinking feeling in the pit of my stomach."*

Use the feeling as information. What could the sinking feeling be trying to tell you?

### Consult Aaron Feuerstein

In Lawrence, Massachusetts, just before Christmas of 1995, most of a large family-owned business named Malden Mills burned to the ground. The owner, Aaron Feuerstein, faced a tough choice. He could take the $300 million in insurance money and retire in comfort to Florida or build a new factory in another country like his competitors. Instead, he chose to rebuild the factory in Lawrence.

But Feuerstein went well beyond his commitment to keep jobs in the community. He spent over $25 million to pay his 3,000 employees with full benefits for the months it took to rebuild. The convictions that guided him were clear. He acknowledged the religious teachings of his Jewish tradition and how they instilled in him an obligation to treat workers honorably. *"I consider our workers an asset, not an expense."* His clear, values-based decision not only honored his family's long relationship with company employees and their families but also earned him the respect and admiration of his community. He received twelve honorary degrees and numerous humanitarian awards, was lionized in national newspapers and business magazines, and was invited to be the president's honored guest for the State of the Union Address. He was variously described as a mensch, a role model of responsible business ownership, and a shining example of compassionate leadership.

Whom do you respect, living or dead, who could serve as your wise counselor?

*"If you were me, and [the guiding values] mattered most to you, what would you do?"*

### Draw the Problem

It can be helpful to set the problem in front of you visually. Use a white board, an easel pad, or a pad of paper to write down the guiding values and the available options. Then, look at them in relationship to the guiding values in several different ways.

First, conduct a side-by-side comparison. If there are a number of options, it may be difficult to compare and assess them as a list. The technique described in Chapter 3, "Paired Comparison Analysis," can be used here to sharpen the assessment by isolating a pair of options for review. One variation of this technique requires that you rank each pair by assigning a score. Then you aggregate the scores to determine which option best fits the guiding values overall when compared to other options one at a time. A simple scoring format is:

3 = far superior to the other
2 = superior to the other
1 = marginally superior to the other
0 = no better than the other.

Second, when you have time and the situation is appropriate, consider making a decision matrix with options listed on the left side and criteria at the top of columns. Apply each important value to each option in turn, and assess how well the option satisfies the value:

3 = satisfies this value at a high level
2 = satisfies this value at a moderate level
1 = satisfies this value somewhat
0 = does not satisfy this value.

Then score each option according to how well it satisfies a range of important values.

For more ways to draw the problem see the "Decision Matrix" and "Balance Sheet" worksheets in the Appendix.

### If You Are on Your Own. . .

Follow the same directions.

### *Embrace the Downside*

The goal: Acknowledge the aspects of the decision that the decision-maker does not like, does not want, or wishes could be different—and consider what will result from each.

There is a natural tendency to skip over the parts of the decision that make you uncomfortable. Most of us want to feel good about what we do. We also care about how others see us. It feels risky to admit the imperfect aspects of the decision. If you are in a group or a team, remind participants that this step helps prepare for possible criticism. It also protects the decision-maker's credibility with stakeholders. If a decision-maker is not prepared to inform others that he has carefully weighed these problems, he looks careless, incompetent, or callous. This requires courage and intellectual honesty. Every tough decision has a downside. Own up to it.

### Remove the Emperor's Clothes

When a group or individual is invested in a decision as good and honorable, it is possible to dress it up and fail to see the decision as others will. Think of the risks and consequences that others may experience or perceive.

"Okay. We've examined this from every angle, and it's not fair to hold up Dr. Seraphy's application any longer. He certainly appears to be rehabilitated, and he comes to us with stellar credentials and references—equaling or exceeding our normal standards for acceptance. He also comes with some heavy baggage. Because this is his hometown and because of the horrific nature of his crime, many of our employees and patients are apprehensive—even angry—about the prospect of having him on staff. So, morale is an issue, which in turn affects our ability to provide first-rate treatment. In turning him down, we aren't ruining his life. Dr. Seraphy can practice elsewhere. We at Bethany Memorial have to go on with our mission here in Capital City. This is an unfortunate situation all around. Speaking selfishly, I wish he'd stayed put in Chicago."

"Now that we have decided to reject Dr. Seraphy's application, we have to think hard about whom this is going to hurt and the criticism we can anticipate."

Weighing the risks associated with each option can be productive, although predicting consequences for a course of action is not always easy. Classifying risk as unlikely, possible, or likely may be helpful in assessing a risk's significance.

### Put Your Good Name on It

For years, *Good Housekeeping* magazine has put its seal of approval on products that measure up to its standards. There is power in considering whether you would place your own seal of approval on the choice you are making. If you write down all of the intended and positive elements of the decision and include a clear statement of the likely and possible downsides, can you sign your name to a statement at the end?

*"After considering all of the above aspects of this decision, I, Mark Bennett, approve it as the best possible choice at this time."*

### Ask an Angel of Reality

Whom do you know who is intelligent, trustworthy, and candid? People making tough decisions need to keep as much perspective as possible throughout the process. When a decision road winds through the thicket of facts, opinions, intentions, values, and consequences, it is easy to become so close to all of the elements that you can't see the whole. Seek a reality check from someone who will level with you.

*"Jim, we asked you to step in and be a sounding board for the committee. We'd like to lay out our conclusion and the reasoning that we used to get us there. We'll give you our best assessment of the weaknesses of our decision and the negative impacts we foresee. We're counting on you to ask the tough questions and tell us how it looks to you. Please don't hold back!"*

### If You Are on Your Own. . .

You can follow the directions for the first two recommendations. However, a true "angel of reality" has a perspective that is different from yours.

Without someone to play this critical role, listen to your own inner voice of doubt about the decision outcome you hope for. What does your inner "angel of reality" say? Is it worth listening to?

**Remember:**
- Make it a real choice that you own by stepping toward what is important rather than away from what you don't like.
- Others will see the downside.
- Take the time to be creative and resourceful.

See the "Worksheet for Step 4: Choose to Act" in the Appendix.

**Consider another story about a difficult decision at work. . .**

Jane Fredericks is a dedicated employee of a social service agency who faces competing loyalties within her professional and personal lives. As you read the story, ask yourself the following questions:

- What are her options?
- What do you imagine matters most? Which option does that value support?
- What consequences are likely because of this choice?

> Jane Fredericks is a caseworker with a special program for rape victims, run by the district court. Her role is to act as an advocate for the victims, providing emotional support and being available to help or get help whenever a victim calls. Jane carries a pager so the victims on her caseload can reach her at any time. Some are desperate—battling severe depression and harboring suicidal thoughts. Just two weeks ago, a woman on a colleague's caseload committed suicide one week before she was to testify at trial. Due to the demands of the job, Jane works nights and weekends to keep up with the caseload and always goes the extra mile for her clients. This is more than a job. It's a mission. In college, a close friend was raped and dropped out of school. Jane saw firsthand the anguish a victim goes through. She often forms deep personal ties with her clients.
>
> Jane hasn't taken a real vacation in over two years—only a day off here and there. For the past year she has planned an out-of-state family reunion for her parents' fiftieth wedding anniversary. Jane, her parents, and her four siblings will be together for the first time in over a decade. The vacation has been scheduled for many months. Because the family lives in different parts of the country, it has been difficult to get everyone to commit, but she finally got it together. Last week, the caseworker who was going to look after her clients during her vacation was in a serious auto accident and is still hospitalized. Jane's boss just came in to her office and begged her to reconsider her plans. There is no one else who can fill in. Jane's boss is already covering other trials during the same period. Two of Jane's clients are particularly fragile, and both will be going to trial during the planned absence.

# 5

## Communicate Transparently

*The highest duty and the highest proof of wisdom—that deed and word should be in accord.*

**Seneca the Younger**

We live in a society and a time where secrets flourish. Whether in the name of national security, political advantage, family harmony, or competitive business interests, we shy away from openness. We are reluctant to admit mistakes or disappointments.

This chapter emphasizes respect and candor when communicating decisions, perhaps the most provocative of all our recommendations. Good decisions that are poorly explained routinely go off track. If all you see is a decision without explanation, you comprehend it much as you would an iceberg by viewing only its tip. Without clear understanding of the underlying structure, you can only imagine the rest.

**Breaking story from today's *Calloway Star Reporter*...**

In a press conference held this morning at Metro Medical Center, CEO Ralph Wallerstein announced that he was rejecting an offer of a fully equipped van to provide medical services to underserved, rural communities in Calloway County over the next five years. "I can't begin to express my gratitude to Bill Leckerson and Leckerson Dodge for their generous offer. It is with great sadness that I have decided not to accept their donation."

Wallerstein went on to explain that, were he to accept the van, he would have to eliminate an already promised, first-ever bonus to employees. "Let me tell you why—and what I don't like about my decision," Wallerstein said. "Our mission and tradition demand that we serve the poor, and this van would certainly help us accomplish that mission. Last year our board of trustees identified expanding services to rural populations as a top priority. This van would move us solidly in that direction. During the week since Bill Leckerson made the offer I've met with staff, administration, and board members to discuss the facts and conditions and to get their input. There is no doubt that the van would provide much-needed primary care to underserved people in the county. However, the qualifying factor of the gift is that Metro would need to cover the van's operating costs, excluding maintenance, and we would need to commit the funds up front. Unfortunately, hiring and providing benefits for medical staff, technicians, and qualified van operators would take all the funds we have available—funds that have been set aside for employee bonuses for having met and exceeded budget expectations for the first time in seven years. It's my understanding that if Metro declines this offer, Meals on Wheels will accept the van and cover the first year's expenses."

Following the press conference, Wallerstein further clarified his decision. "What's most important to me, as CEO, is that I keep my promises to our loyal, hard-working staff. As vital as the van could be to expand our mission, our staff lives our mission every day. For that reason, I am declining the van. It's equally important to me that the community understands what went into my decision. I hope I've explained this as clearly and completely as possible. Thank you."

Our fifth and final challenge on the road to a good decision is about being accountable—that is, being responsible and answerable for our decisions. Even when we have undeniable legal and moral authority to decide and act on our own, our decisions involve and affect others. Are we willing to stand behind our decisions? Will the people who deserve to know the details receive a direct, honest account? Will we acknowledge the negative impacts of our decisions, whether intended or unintended? Only through clear and honest communication with those affected can we be accountable and establish credibility.

Decision-makers come in all shapes and sizes: city mayors and state governors; CEOs of Fortune 500 corporations and heads of small businesses; board chairs and directors of schools, churches, and social service agencies. Regardless of their different positions and scope of authority, decision-makers have much in common—including reluctance if not refusal to see candid communication as essential to the decision-making process.

> *A decision is responsible when the group that makes it has to answer for it to those who are directly or indirectly affected by it.*
> **Charles Frankel**

They justifiably claim with confidence that they make their decisions honorably, based on their most important values. *"We may not have worked to understand perspective and identify the range of stakeholder values as thoroughly as we might. But when we make good decisions—and we do—we are clear about and committed to what matters."* These same decision-makers also lament that people often misunderstand or criticize their decisions, especially when the choices are painful. *"The ink isn't dry before the attacks begin. No one cuts us any slack. It's lonely at the top."*

Failure to communicate well, if at all, is the usual culprit. Without an explanation, a decision's real, multilayered meaning remains hidden.

Consider a decision about whether to end medical life-support treatment. The final decision may come down to a simple *yes* or *no*. However, such a decision has little meaning without understanding the key participants and the process leading up to it. In the case of Metro Medical Center, either it will accept the van or it will not. For the decision to gain any traction, however, the participants' struggle and the decision's depth and breadth need the light of day. Good decisions thrive on clarity and openness.

When decision-makers do not tell an adequate, genuine story about the decision, others make up their own. Count on at least three stories for every decision. First, there is the real story of the decision-making process, the one that features a decision's actual reasons. Second, there is the story that the decision-maker tells others. Third, there is the story that others pass along or that they tell themselves. A decision-maker serves her own cause by making sure the first and second stories are the same. She can also do much to preempt the creation of competing stories with a complete, credible telling of the real story.

The previous chapters described techniques for being comprehensive and coherent in our decision-making:

- We are **comprehensive** when our report demonstrates that we did our homework, consulted the right people to understand the full range of values, and did not rush to judgment.

- We are **coherent** when the stated basis for our decision, that is, the values that really guided it, aligns with the decision and makes sense to others—even if they do not agree with our top values.

In this chapter, we add **transparency** as the third quality necessary for a decision to have integrity and succeed. We are transparent when we reveal the real basis for a decision rather than spin a version designed to conceal or divert attention. A decision explained well always contains the **essential elements of communicating**. Finally, we prepare you to promote openness by understanding the barriers of **secrecy** that keep the decision's real story under wraps.

## WHY TRANSPARENCY?

To be credible decision-makers we must be truthful, believable, and accountable to those who have a stake in the decision. For an important decision to succeed, the visible product at the end of the process must be a

# Elements of Integrity

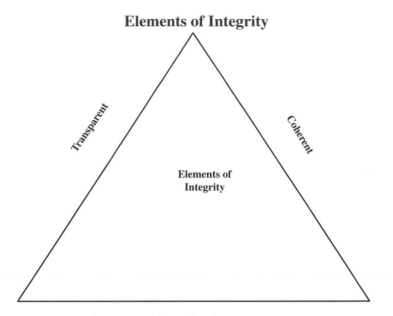

clear, genuine report to those owed an explanation. This explanation is incomplete and inadequate if it fails to include a summary of what happened and why the action was taken.

Our focus here is on the end of the

> *To be persuasive we must be believable; to be believable we must be credible; to be credible we must be truthful.*
> **Edward R. Murrow**

story. Does the CEO's candid reporting enhance his credibility in the hospital and the community? Or does his focus on the decision's downside simply give his critics more ammunition?

Assume the decision-making process, while difficult, was thorough. Everyone knew from the start that the CEO would make the final decision. He consulted stakeholders, considered a number of different perspectives, identified and discussed the range of applicable values, and assured that he and his decision-making colleagues weighed competing values and advocated for what each deemed most important.

Before the press conference, CEO Ralph Wallerstein called an all-staff meeting.

"Thank you all for coming this afternoon. I want you to be the first to know my decision concerning the van, and I want you to hear it from me directly. While all of you know at least part of the story, let me start from the beginning. A week ago, Bill Leckerson approached the chair of our board of trustees with a very generous offer. Leckerson Dodge wants to donate a fully equipped van with an estimated value of up to $250,000, for use by a local nonprofit organization. They came to us first. The conditions of the offer were that Leckerson Dodge would donate the van and all necessary maintenance for the life of the five-year project, an additional contribution worth about $35,000. Except for maintenance, the recipient must pay for all operating costs and 'must have the funds available to commit now.' Bill Leckerson informed me that if Metro could not accept the donation, Calloway County Meals on Wheels would take it as a mobile kitchen to deliver food to homebound persons. Bill wanted an answer within a week.

> *You must study to be frank with the world; frankness is the child of honesty and courage.*
>
> **Robert E. Lee**

As you know, for several years we have identified serving Calloway County's underserved rural population as a top priority. It's been our primary strategic goal for some time now. I needed help with this decision, so I asked some of you to form teams to investigate the issues, listen to as many stakeholders as possible, and identify the most important values. I want to thank Rosemary Chavez, our chief financial officer, oncology nurse Jim Lewis, outpatient co-ordinator Ron Willis, and housekeeping manager Lois White. Thanks for taking this on.

Here is what Rosemary, Jim, Ron, and Lois told me. They held three employee forums this past week, to cover all three shifts. They talked individually and in groups with staff, managers, and community health professionals. By the end of the week, it was clear that:

- No current funds are available except the money we have set aside to pay the employee bonus.
- Monies are available after this year, and if we could see a way to support year one, the van could have a dental room in addition to its health functions, and could reach 4,000 patient visits per year.
- Employee polls conducted at each forum yielded the same nearly fifty-fifty split. Half responded, 'Keep your promise about the bonus.' The other half said, 'Use the money to serve underserved populations.'

You all identified a number of relevant issues, including fostering good community relations, being responsible stewards of our resources, following our strategic plan, providing quality patient care, and taking care not to overextend. However, your top two values by far were: keeping promises made directly to employees, and providing care to the underserved as promised in our mission statement. Clearly, I can't fully honor both. I had to choose between two very important values. I realize that, because of my decision, critical health needs of many people in our county will remain unaddressed. I wouldn't pass up this opportunity unless it was more important to me, and to Metro, to keep the promise I made to you last year. You kept your end of the bargain by meeting and often exceeding budget expectations. Therefore, I am keeping my word. I will distribute the employee bonus this year, as promised. I am proud of our employees. While we still hope to do more, I know you bring our mission alive every day.

I also want you to know that tomorrow I'm holding a press conference to make this decision public. Are there any questions?"

What would have been the effect if, instead of giving a candid and personal report to all staff, Wallerstein had chosen to send a memo to management? *"Thank you for your input on the medical van issue. We have decided to decline the donation and distribute the employee bonus as originally promised. Please inform your staff about this decision."* What if he had elected not to issue a public announcement but instead alerted his management team to be prepared to answer questions from the press, should they arise? *"Let's let sleeping dogs lie. Divulge as little as possible. Don't volunteer any more information than is absolutely necessary. No need to stir up controversy where there isn't any. If you have questions, the PR team has some talking points for you."* The CEO chose the road of full accountability through direct, transparent communication. Now let's look at the specific building blocks of effective communication.

> Sometimes, to be silent is to lie.
> **Miguel Unanamo**

## ELEMENTS OF COMMUNICATING

Decisions reported well, that is, explained clearly to those who have a need or a right to hear, feature three elements:

- The report defines the decision clearly and succinctly and identifies who made the decision.
- The report describes, in everyday language appropriate to the situation, the value(s) that drove the decision.
- The decision-maker acknowledges the downside, including important values not honored, as well as people likely to suffer from the decision.

Wallerstein did all of the above. He owned the decision as the final decision-maker, and he named those who helped him by gathering information or consulting during the process. He described his approach with enough detail so people could understand what happened. He explained who participated, what key information was uncovered, and what people said mattered to them. He focused on values, named a number of them, acknowledged the primary conflict, and explained why he was guided by one value more than others.

There was a clear, authentic connection between his top value (keeping a promise) and his decision to pay the bonus and forgo the important opportunity presented by the van. He was concise and candid about the downside of his decision: those value(s) not honored and those individuals and groups hurt by his decision.

CEO Ralph Wallerstein announced that he was turning down an offer of a fully equipped van to provide medical services to underserved, rural communities of Calloway County over the next five years. Far too often we leave a meeting or press conference wondering just what the decision was. *"Are we getting a raise or not?"* *"Is there going to be a layoff?"* We also wonder who actually made the decision. *"We have decided that. . ."* does not reveal who is responsible and accountable. *"I, as CEO, decided that. . ."* *"My leadership team and I have decided to. . ."* *"My team for this decision, included Rosemary, Jim, Ron, and Lois. . . ."* A good report states the decision clearly and identifies who owns the decision.

By clarifying, choosing, and committing, a decision-maker settles on his guiding values and makes a conscious choice. What remains is to communicate effectively. Effective communication explains the final values analysis, avoids jargon, and demonstrates a clear connection between the stated value(s) and the decision. *"I commit myself to keeping the promise I made to you last year. You kept your end of the bargain, met, and often exceeded budget expectations. Therefore, I am keeping my word. I will distribute the employee bonus this year, as promised."* Too often, decision-makers insert values language for tactical reasons, to sell a decision instead of explaining it. No amount of carefully packaged communication can completely camouflage a disingenuous account.

Conversely, although a presentation is inelegant and awkward, if it is honest, it rings true. Its authenticity builds credibility and attracts support.

We are tempted to move away from straight talk into limited tactical communication, so that others will accept our decision. By manipulating audience perceptions, we hope to avoid unfair criticism from hostile stakeholders. What we lose, of course, is our credibility.

Accountability and honest explanations go hand in hand. Good decisions require transparency. The audience for the explanation must be able to see and understand the connection between the announced values and the choice made. When this coherence is missing, anyone with a bit of common sense notices an unmistakable odor. People can disagree and still respect the decision-maker's integrity: *"That's not what I would have done, but I see why you want to go in a different direction."*

> *You don't have to be an ichthyologist to know when a fish stinks.*
> **Daniel Ellsberg**

This is our most important recommendation, and it is the most challenging. We urge a candid, complete accounting of a decision's downside. *"There are some things about this decision I don't like."* *"I realize*

> A weak man has doubts
> before a decision, a strong
> man has them afterwards.
>                    **Karl Kraus**

that, because of my decision, the health needs of many people in our county will remain unaddressed." The issue is not whether there is a downside. All tough decisions shortchange something that matters to someone. How candid are we willing to be in acknowledging what values remain unfulfilled? How open are we in identifying those whom our decision may hurt?

Another form of flawed communication that fails the challenge of accountability is ignoring the downside or soft-pedaling negative consequences. It is natural to avoid the discomfort that comes from acknowledging necessary but harmful effects of a decision. We would much rather stress the positives; even indulge in some wishful thinking. *"Maybe it won't be so bad."*

If a decision-maker is not candid about the downside, the presentation of the decision might look something like the emperor in his new clothes. Others see the naked reality, while he acts as if he's fully dressed. Acknowledging the negative impact of a choice, as well as one's regrets, protects credibility. It may even enhance personal reputation, showing oneself as an individual of integrity who faces tough decisions directly.

## STANDING AGAINST SECRECY

Regrettably, communication that supports accountability is more the exception than the rule. We live in a time and environment where secrecy flourishes. The headlines are filled with examples such as the USA Patriot Act, Enron, and the Catholic Church. Pick up any newspaper for yet another story of controversy rooted in the keeping of secrets.

Most of us have experienced the pressure to keep silent, to hold back from speaking candidly about what we believe. We may remain silent even in the relatively private space of a small group or family considering a decision. We find ourselves limiting communication or slipping into total silence when weighing how much, or how little, to reveal to certain stakeholders.

Through the work of activist Internet bloggers, investigative journalists, anonymous government sources, kiss-and-tell biographers, or whistle-blowers, the truth, or some version of it, usually emerges. When it does, the cost in legal liability, damaged or destroyed reputations, and dashed careers can be substantial. Keeping secrets is, in the end, often impossible.

> God protect me from
> self-interest masquerading
> as moral principle.
>                    **Mark Twain**

To work toward transparency, we must understand the forces that motivate people to keep secrets. There is power in the way things are. To promote openness and accountability, we must be willing to challenge the status quo and overcome certain dynamics and behaviors.

Forces for secrecy fall into two major categories. First, there are our fears that openness will place someone or something important to us at risk. Second are our beliefs about ourselves in the world, which influence how we behave in our families, workplaces, and communities. Think of these fears and beliefs as barriers that conspire to maintain business as usual.

Consider the following four fears:

- **Retaliation**—Will we experience what many whistle-blowers and truth-tellers do—exclusion, personal attacks, or punishment in various forms?

- **Opposition**—If we level with people by talking about a decision's downside, will we be giving ammunition to those who might work againstus?

- **Response to Bad News**—When openness requires that we tell people, face to face, that our decisions will hurt them, how will they react?

> *If one is to do good, it must be done in the minute particulars. The general good is the plea of the hypocrite, the flatterer, and the scoundrel.*
>
> **William Blake**

- **Loss of Esteem**—If others understand the truth about the decision, including negative effects, will they criticize and judge us negatively?

Fear that harm might come to something or someone we care about motivates us to avoid openness. Pervasive beliefs support these fears and reinforce the instinct to hold back the truth.

Many people make a living advising others how to communicate effectively. The belief that effective communication must be tactical shapes behavior and can lead away from honesty and directness. The typical advice is: even if a decision has a downside and we know the real reason for our choice, perhaps it is more professional or more likely to enhance our image if we carefully polish our presentation for each audience, avoiding or downplaying what is likely to upset them.

In organizations, families, and communities, you will find people who believe that honesty isn't worth the trouble, because it doesn't make any difference. Why speak up when management exhibits indifference to the views of employees, partners, and stakeholders? Why deal with the tension and discomfort that truth brings, when your sisters haven't listened to you in the past? When the last two neighborhood meetings ended in pointless arguments, why should it be any different this time?

The belief that time is a scarce commodity also cuts against openness and honesty. This view suggests that it's not necessary, or at least it's unrealistic, to think that we can assemble enough people for a thorough discussion that is worth the time and energy.

Finally, there is a belief that security comes from holding on to information. Keeping information to ourselves and refraining from sharing it with others, especially competitors and adversaries, seems to keep us powerful and protected, despite evidence to the contrary of collapsing governments, presidencies, and corporations.

As you read this list of fears and beliefs that prevent openness, consider your own experiences in organizations, groups, and families. Ask yourself two questions:

- Do these barriers resonate with your experience?
- Can you imagine ways to confront them at home, at work, and in the community?

> *Who you are speaks so loudly, I can't hear a word you're saying.*
> **Ralph Waldo Emerson**

To stand against secrecy and advocate for openness, we must also address an insidious pattern—oversimplifying complex issues. We wage abortion wars, debate privacy and national security, argue the merits of privatizing social security, dispute and define the wisdom of a preemptive foreign policy, and avoid at all (political) costs proposing reinstituting the draft—too often with simplistic appeals to one-dimensional values. These are complicated issues with multiple and mutually exclusive values vying for the lead. Insisting on simplicity merely perpetuates the delusion. Decisions made and explained simplistically may reassure us in the short run, but they frequently fail to thrive. We underestimate the level of mistrust that greets anything less than honest communication.

The abundance of calculated, often disingenuous communication has created a high level of cynicism in the workplace, in government, and in the media. The popular cartoon strip *Dilbert*, by Scott Adams, ruthlessly mines this mother lode of discontent, lampooning every dimension of current organizational life, especially bureaucratic tendencies toward doublespeak, manipulation, and hidden agendas. In a strip titled "Business Language Explained," *"We have to be more competitive,"* translates to, *"Say goodbye to salary increases,"* and, *"We're reengineering your function,"* really means, *"Polish up your resume and prepare to hit the road."* Much of what we hear today, we assume is either false or only partially true. We have come to expect that announcements of important decisions deliberately withhold significant information.

Lack of candor is often intentional. In its benign form, it reflects a decision-maker's fear that truth-telling is inappropriate or unwise. In its more pernicious form, it becomes spin. Spin is the deliberate tailoring of the story behind a decision to serve a partially or completely concealed agenda, at the expense of honesty and integrity. Spin is now a highly compensated skill in politics, advertising, and media relations. "Spin-meisters" attempt to mold opinions with carefully crafted communication, offering reasons for the decision that have little if anything to do with its real motivation or driving values. They are concerned only with the immediate impact of the message. *"How will it play?" "Will it grab their attention?" "Will it quiet the outcry?" "Will the polls react favorably?"*

> *Look, I've done it their way this far and now it's my turn. I'm my own handler. Any questions? Ask me... There's not going to be any more handler stories because I'm the handler. I'm Doctor Spin.*
> **Dan Quayle**

The decision's downside, the people who will be hurt, or the values the decision violates or sets aside receive no mention. A mayor's announcement to float a bond issue for a new downtown stadium will focus on positive projections for economic benefit. There will be little or no mention of residents forced to move from their homes, the months of traffic disruption, or the loss of business by small merchants during construction. Decision-makers who do not level with us may ultimately doom their projects. Decisions reported in this less-than-honest manner regularly wither or spin out of control.

## WHAT YOU CAN DO

### Touch All the Bases

The goal: Develop a comprehensive and coherent decision, where transparent reporting becomes the final step toward accountability.

A decision succeeds when the decision-maker has done his homework and when he builds in accountability throughout the process. The formula for successful decision-making is: create a comprehensive and coherent decision then communicate these qualities as honestly and transparently as possible.

### Own the Decision

From the beginning of the decision-making process through the final report, be clear about whose decision it is. *"My management team met with staff to gather their input. In the end, it was my decision. I have made my decision. Not everyone will agree, so let me explain the range of values and different interests I heard and my reasons for deciding as I did." "The leadership council made this decision. Council members who participated are. . . . In the end, the decision was unanimous."*

### Know and Show Your Cards

There is a reason you decided as you did. Come clean and explain the "why" behind what you decided. *"You all identified a number of values that are important, including fostering good community relations, being responsible stewards of our resources, following our strategic plan, providing quality patient care, and taking care not to overextend. By far, your top two values were keeping promises made directly to employees and providing care to the underserved, as promised in our mission statement. Clearly, I can't fully honor both. I have to choose between two very important values. I have done so."*

### Honor the Downside

Do not merely allude to or rush past the decision's downside. Linger. You are speaking to people who may not agree with you, who may have told you so, and who need to hear that you have paid attention. *"Let me tell you what I don't like about my decision. Our mission and tradition demand that we serve the poor. This van would help us accomplish our mission. Last year our board of trustees identified expanding services to rural populations as a top priority. This van would move us solidly in that direction. My decision postpones that commitment. Underserved people will continue to be underserved."*

### *Audience, Audience, Audience*

The goal: Identify those who need or deserve to hear your decision. Prepare an appropriately comprehensive and clear account of your decision and your reasons with your audience in mind.

Usually, people other than the decision-maker have been involved in creating the decision. Nearly always, the decision affects a number of people. These individuals and groups have a right to hear and understand what was decided. Not only is it the right thing to do, it is also prudent. Disaffected audiences are masters at boycott and sabotage.

### Remember What They Want to Know

You may need support, approval, or cooperation from those who will implement or be affected by your decision. You need to know who they are and what matters to them. If you consulted them, you also should demonstrate that you listened to their ideas and concerns. *"We surveyed all employees to take the pulse of their opinions. The equally divided results did not confirm a choice that would provide high satisfaction throughout the organization. Therefore, we returned to our mission and core values to guide us."*

Your report should feature their role and contribution to the decision-making process. *"We will continue to seek and use employee input on a variety of important issues. My management team and I will be facing more*

*tough choices in our health care environment. You are our partners, and it*
*helps to know what you think."*

### Adjust the Format to Fit Your Style and the Situation

Your personal style and the reporting environment should dictate the format. Note that CEO Ralph Wallerstein used the bottom-line approach in his press conference. If it is most important that the audience hear the decision, then lead with a crisp statement of your decision. After starting with the decision, explain the guiding values and then address the downside. In closing, it is often useful to repeat the decision.

If you are concerned that, once hearing the decision, the audience will not give your reasoning the attention you want, make them wait. To do this, consider the story format. When you tell the decision as a story, this has the advantage of building to the decision by emphasizing the process that led up to it. Some decision-makers want their audience to pay attention until the end. When Wallerstein addressed his staff, he used a story approach:

How you approached this decision. *"While all of you know at least a part of this story, let me start from the beginning."*

What steps you took. *"I asked some of you to form a team to investigate the issues, listen to as many stakeholders as possible, and identify the values important to them. I want to thank Rosemary Chavez, our chief financial officer, oncology nurse Jim Lewis, outpatient coordinator Ron Willis, and housekeeping manager Lois White. Thanks for taking this on."*

Continue to develop the downside of your choice. Finally, land on the value(s) that drove your decision and use the decision as a punch line. *"It became clear that important things that matter were in tension. We struggled with the impact of further delays in adding this vital service to our mission. We recognize that some people will continue to suffer from lack of care. However, keeping our promise to our employees is like bedrock. Your belief in our integrity is the foundation for our mission and our survival as an organization. You bring our mission alive every day."*

### Resist the Siren Song to Gloss Over the Downside or Lessen the Impact with Half-hearted Promises

Be careful with talk about mitigating the downside. Much of what tries to look like a heartfelt commitment to address the negative impacts falls short of credible mitigation. Over-promising and under-delivering undermine credibility. Those likely to bear the brunt of the decision may interpret statements about minimizing impact as an attempt to whitewash the harm they foresee. If so, they may perceive your mitigation efforts as disrespectful or insincere, even though that was not your intent.

You respect your audience and stakeholders when you talk straight and acknowledge the negative while upholding the positive effects of your decision. When there is a genuine commitment to do something to reduce or redress negative impacts, be sure to avoid:

General statements of intention (*"I'll make it a priority that this will never happen again on my watch."*)

Hollow empathy (*"I know this is tough for you and your families."*)

Feel-good comments designed to minimize suffering (*"If we all pull together it won't be so bad."*)

Half-baked ideas (*"Maybe the employee morale committee could consider whether to brainstorm some possible options to address. I'll try to pull some people together soon."*)

See "Mitigating Downside Impacts" in the Appendix.

### Stand Tall

The goal: Communicate, openly and directly, the scope and justification for your decision, despite powerful forces against doing so.

Effective decision-makers align their decisions with key values and consider their work unfinished unless they have communicated clearly with those affected. Decision-makers who fail to either align or communicate their decisions are sloppy. Those who align but do not communicate lack follow-through. Those who carefully package poorly aligned decisions focus on spin. Highly credible decision-makers create and clearly communicate decisions that align closely with their key values.

### Bring Fear out of the Shadows

We fear retaliation, opposition, and people's response to bad news. We may also be concerned about liability, competitive advantage, and loss of esteem. Antidotes to these fears include commitment to truth, credibility in the eyes of those who disagree with us, and defusing the opposition by acknowledging its arguments.

### Treat Beliefs as Assumptions to Be Tested

In organizational, public, and personal life, most of us have felt the pressure to keep silent. A number of stated or unstated beliefs support the status quo and resist openness and the expression of nonconforming opinions. Irving Janis, the author of *Groupthink*, refers to these beliefs as "mind-guards."

Consider invoking the following list of counter-beliefs to challenge the internal and external voices calling for something less than candor:

- A difficult choice always has a downside.
- A highly polished presentation will not keep others from seeing the downside.
- Less than open communication feeds a cycle of cynicism that erodes credibility and trust.
- Credibility and trust are precious assets, like money in the bank.
- Power and security built on secrecy are fragile, as evidenced by the collapse of governments, presidencies, and corporations over the years.
- It is easy to be overconfident about our own judgment and to underestimate the value of input from others.
- Decision-makers become stronger and more capable when they listen well to others.
- Rarely is there sufficient information or data to transform a tough choice into an easy one. The trade-off between important and conflicting values remains.

### Test Your Communication with a Tough Trial Audience

If the decision is important and you have the time, make a dry run. Pick one or more trusted people who were not involved in your decision to serve as a trial audience. Ask them to give you clear, no-holds-barred feedback on your proposed communication.

Make sure they answer three challenge questions about the integrity of the decision.

*"Have I been open enough about the basis for my decision and honest about what I don't like about it?"* (**Transparent**)

*"Have I demonstrated that I considered what matters to stakeholders?"* (**Comprehensive**)

*"Do the stated reasons for the decision clearly connect with the choice made so others understand?"* (**Coherent**)

Anticipate the *"Yes, buts..."* from your audience. What doubts and concerns might they have? If you don't know, is there anyone you can ask? What are the key values you couldn't honor? No report can win over every critic and naysayer. However, a clear, candid account usually leaves those who disagree with the view that you made your decision in good faith based on legitimate differences about what is most important.

**Remember:**
- Whenever possible, go directly to your audience(s) and explain.
- Let in the sunshine.
- Do not squander the power of a good decision by failing to communicate well.

See the "Worksheet for Step 5: Communicate Transparently" in the Appendix.

**Reconsider a story. . .**

In Chapter 3, you read the story *Health Insurance: For Some or All?*—a story about Integrated Management Systems and Ruby Romero. Theresa reported the management committee's recommendation to the CEO, Jane Blaisdell. Now, Jane has some important choices to make about communicating this decision. If you were in her shoes, how would you close out this decision-making process?

Review the story and ask yourself:

- Who are Jane Blaisdell's audiences? How should she describe the process to them?
- Who needs to hear about the decision?
- Who stands to lose? Be specific.
- What key points should her decision report contain? Be specific. Create your own script.
- Would your message change for different audiences? Explain.

For a review of the five steps and techniques for moving through them, see "Moving through the Steps" in the Appendix.

# Part II

## Difficult Terrain

# 6

---

# Avoid Mental and Emotional Detours

---

*Only as you do know yourself can your brain serve you as a sharp and efficient tool. Know your own failings, passions, and prejudices so you can separate them from what you see. Know also when you actually have thought through to the nature of the thing with which you are dealing and when you are not thinking at all.*

Bernard Baruch

Even with a sense of the road ahead, it is possible to lose our way. The map is not the territory. Some twists and turns are unforeseeable. Conditions are subject to change. In the first part of the book, we mapped the road that leads to good decisions. Now let's turn our attention to some of the obstacles and detours that may appear along the way.

Among the rapidly changing conditions that lead us astray are certain patterns of thought and emotion. We naturally wish to protect something that is precious to us or move toward our dreams. We hope. We fear. If we fail to pay attention, however, our thoughts and emotions may diminish the clarity and understanding we need to create a good decision.

This chapter offers some guidance for **understanding human nature** in terms of our perceptions and emotions. It then describes ways to spot wrong turns that **lead us astray**. Finally, the "What You Can Do" section provides **navigational aids** to help avoid detours or get back on the road after taking a wrong turn.

## THE WINDFALL?

**A bit of history:** John, MaryAnn, and Toby are the adult children and sole heirs of Larry Gandalfo, a Portland businessman who died unexpectedly three months ago. Gandalfo, the son of Italian immigrants, was a self-made success, rising from a low-end construction laborer to become a reputable builder of quality custom homes. Dynamic, energetic, and something of a maverick, Gandalfo had always been tight-lipped about his financial affairs, and after a frustrating, ultimately fruitless search for a will, the three siblings turned for advice to a prominent local attorney—their Uncle Phillip.

It would be hard to imagine three more different individuals than Gandalfo's trio of children. John is forty-three, single, and childless. As the oldest (and only son), he was the first in his family to attend college, eventually earned an MBA, and is now a wealthy real estate developer. MaryAnn, forty-one, is a high-school dropout and recovering alcoholic. An early marriage was an emotional and financial disaster. Now, she and her second husband (also a recovering alcoholic) struggle to raise their three-year-old daughter on hourly wage salaries that barely cover food and rent. The youngest, Toby, is thirty-eight, married with five children. Her husband, a mechanical engineer, has a solid job with good benefits. She has elected to be a stay-at-home mom. Still, with college for five looming in the future, most of their money goes into savings and there's little left over for extras. Perhaps because of his education and a closer relationship with his father, only John has shown an interest in learning or entering the family business.

**The first meeting with the attorney.** Phillip: "Well guys, I have a surprise for you. As you know, Williams Brothers Custom Homes has always been your dad's biggest competitor. Yesterday I had a call from Sinclair Williams. It seems they want to buy out Gandalfo Custom Homes, and they have a serious cash offer on the table. I'm recommending you

> *Beware of taking any one thing out its connections, for that way folly lies.*
> **Ralph Waldo Emerson**

consider it carefully, as it offers a fair and uncomplicated way to wind up Larry's affairs. I think I can assure each of you quite a tidy nest egg."


## UNDERSTANDING HUMAN NATURE

When we experience the weight and pressure of a challenging decision, it is easy to get swept up by events and our reactions to them. If you develop your own set of habits for bringing your best thought and creativity to the fore, you can fall back on a trained response in a stressful time. You gain a sense of decisiveness by preparing in advance. Things are more likely to break your way. Although any such set of habits is highly personal, some traps are known and avoidable.

In the past thirty years, lessons from behavioral science researchers have offered insight into the workings of the mind. They help us understand how people behave when they choose and decide. Given the increasing interest in the workings of our brains and emotions, it is not surprising that the 2002 Nobel Prize for Economics went to a psychologist for his groundbreaking research into what influences us when we choose one thing instead of another.

The work of Nobel Laureate Daniel Kahneman and his colleagues in the cognitive sciences shows how bias and other factors shape the way we perceive and understand. While their work in the emerging field of behavioral economics focuses on monetary valuing, their principles can apply to situations where values drive decisions.

Most of their research findings boil down to two ways that our emotions and perceptions deter us from seeing, thinking, and understanding clearly. First, we direct our attention and focus on what is less important, failing to see and pay attention to what is more important. Second, we see, but fail to understand the weight or meaning of what we see.

Consider three core conclusions from behavioral economics:

- **Perceptions influence judgment.** We are emotional creatures whose behavior is guided only partially by reason. This reality formed the basis for Federal Reserve Chairman Alan Greenspan's famous characterization of the stock market euphoria of the late 1990s as "irrational exuberance."

- **People are less rational and more prone to manipulation than they think.** The classic example is that most of us will pay more for a product with a credit card than we will with cash, in spite of the reality that "all dollars spend the same."

- **People of all socioeconomic and education levels repeat the same mistakes.** The intelligence and increased sophistication that come from higher education do not protect against these mistakes in judgment.

> *The more intelligent and cultured a man is, the more subtly he can humbug himself.*
> **Carl Jung**

How might these core principles relate to John, MaryAnn, and Toby as they come to terms with the loss of their father and the prospect of a significant inheritance?

John is confident about money issues. He sees himself as a savvy, successful businessman. He makes important financial decisions all the time, weighs financial risks quickly, and moves forward. He may be most vulnerable to overconfidence.

MaryAnn is still emotionally fragile and almost desperate to gain the inherited resources and escape her hand-to-mouth existence. She has no confidence about financial decision-making. Her vulnerability probably lies in her strong emotional response to the circumstances. The prospects of financial salvation may swamp her ability to consider what is wise.

Like MaryAnn, Toby is relatively inexperienced in financial matters. However, she and her husband have a much more stable situation, emotionally and financially. They are unlikely to be overconfident like John but may have some patterns of relating to financial decisions that are problematic.

| Summary of Larry Gandalfo's Estate | |
|---|---|
| Residence—Fair Market Value (minus selling costs) | $200,000 |
| Personal Property—Proceeds from Estate Sale | $15,000 |
| Gandalfo Custom Homes (sale to Williams) | $700,000 |
| Bank Accounts and IRA | $25,000 |
| Less | |
| − Unpaid income taxes | $10,000 |
| − Estimated legal fees | $5,000 |
| Net Estate to be divided | $925,000 |
| | **(Each receives $308,000+)** |

**The final offer.** Phillip: "Here is a summary of the assets in Larry's estate, including the counter offer from Williams Brothers.

They increased their original offer by 10 percent As you can see, the bulk of the value is in the business. If each of you receives a grand total of $308,000 from the estate, $233,000 of that amount will come from the sale to Williams Brothers. Today, the three of you need to consider your options. I promised to get back to their lawyer by Friday with an answer."

## WHAT LEADS US ASTRAY

Like a navigator seated next to you as you travel down an unfamiliar road, this section helps you anticipate a wrong turn or promptly recognize one soon after you've taken it, so you can get back on track.

> *We made too many wrong mistakes.*
>
> **Yogi Berra**

John: "Phillip, hold on just a second. In the months before he died, Pop and I had a series of conversations. We agreed, in principle, to join forces. The idea was to combine my experience with development and his custom home expertise to develop some subdivisions. I already have an option on a great parcel. What if we keep the business, with each of us having a one-third share? I could run the joint venture, and Pop's construction superintendents would oversee the home building. They have been like Pop's right arm for over twenty years and know the business inside out. I trust them."

Toby and MaryAnn looked at one another but made no immediate response. Finally Phillip broke the silence. "John, you and the girls need to come to a decision that suits all three of you. Your idea suits you but adds a degree of uncertainty for your sisters. The Williams Brothers offer is simple—all cash with no contingencies. You each walk away with an equal share."

John: "I'm saying it's a big mistake to think only in immediate financial terms. There is a bigger picture. Aside from the fact that Pop and I had all but agreed to do this, there are at least three other good reasons to turn down the Williams Brothers offer:

1. If we sell out, some or all of Pop's loyal employees could be laid off or have their salaries and benefits reduced by the new owners. Pop always paid top dollar and really cared about his workers.

2. By continuing to own the business as a family, we honor what Pop created under the family name.

3. We have to assume that Pop's business is worth at least $700,000, and this could be a lowball offer. Besides, my conservative projections on this joint venture show a profit to Gandalfo Custom that could give each one-third owner about $35,000/year over the next five years as we build out the homes in the subdivision. That's $175,000 right there. So my idea produces good income for each of us, plus we retain the business as a valuable asset that we can sell in the future, if we want. If the subdivision goes well, the business could be worth substantially more in a few years."

Let's use some of the principles of behavioral economics to sort out the issues for John, MaryAnn, and Toby.

## Framing Principle

**How a question is posed affects the way we respond.** Pollsters know that the way they ask a question affects the kind of response they receive. You can ask a question with a positive or a negative slant. Or, your question can assume a particular view. One well-known study demonstrating this effect looked at the influence of asking people which medical treatment they would prefer. The question was posed differently to separate groups of doctors, pa-

> *The foolish reject what they see, not what they think; the wise reject what they think, not what they see.*
> **Huang Po**

tients, and graduate students. Researchers asked one group a question framed in terms of a patient's chance of dying: *"Of 100 people having surgery, ten will die during surgery, thirty-two will have died in the first year, and sixty-six will have died at the end of five years. Of 100 people having radiation therapy, none will die during treatment, twenty-three will die within one year, and seventy-eight will die within five years. Which treatment would you prefer?"* They asked the other group the question framed in terms of a patient's chance of living: *"Of 100 people having surgery, ninety will survive the surgery, sixty-eight will survive past one year, and thirty-four will survive through five years. Of 100 people having radiation therapy, all will survive the treatment, seventy-seven will survive one year, and twenty-two will survive past five years. Which treatment would you prefer?"* Although the actual risk was the same in both questions, people's answers were significantly different. Even experts like physicians answered differently, depending on how the question was asked (McNeil et al., 1982).

Like paintings and photographs, decisions look different depending upon how they are framed. Our perspective determines our frame. Chapter 1 described factors such as experience, values, and training that shape this perspective. Frames include and exclude people, options, and information. We need to know our own frame as well as consider alternative ways of looking at the issue. The key is finding an expansive frame that reveals the issues embedded in our decision. We also need to understand how others frame the choice.

> MaryAnn: "Okay—just to clarify things—what is my share of the business if we sell it?"
>
> Phillip: "$233,000. That doesn't include the remaining $75,000 you'll automatically receive from Pop's estate, whether or not we sell the business."

This is an important question, which links to other questions. If we ask, answer, or act on a question out of sequence, we may frame the problem too narrowly. For example, a question more broadly framed would be, *"How does my share of the business, if sold, compare to what I might get if I held on to my share?"*

### Loss Aversion

**We tend to attach greater weight to possible losses than to possible gains.** People feel more pain from loss than pleasure from gain or profit. We are both risk-averse and loss-averse when it comes to gain. Because we would rather have a bird in the hand, we take risks to avoid a loss. This ties in to framing. Framing or posing something as a gain or a loss can change the way many will evaluate the situation. A good process for decision-making will surface potential loss and gain for us to balance. Ironically, because we fear loss, we don't evaluate it thoroughly. If we skip over the downside of a choice, we miss the chance to put it into proper perspective.

> John: "Look, let's lay out our options about the business and look at each of them from the standpoint of gain and loss. You know I want to keep the business. But I've been thinking about this for a while, and I have more experience in the real estate business than you do. So let's test my judgment by taking a hard look at this together."

By holding possible gains and losses in front of us, we have the opportunity to reflect on the way they push and pull us.

**Option—Sell to Williams Brothers**

| Positives/Gain | Negatives/Loss |
|---|---|
| • *Immediate gain of $233,000 each* | • *Loss of potential future profits,* |
| • *Avoids future uncertainties (shared ownership hassles, business risks) Allows each freedom to use money now to meet unique needs* | *amount unknown. . . possible income of $175,000 over five years PLUS still own the business* |
| | • *Loss of identity of family business* |
| | • *Threat to job security of Pop's longtime, loyal employees* |

> *Nothing is as easy as deceiving yourself, for what you wish you readily believe.*
> **Demosthenes**

MaryAnn: "John, I'm sure you are good at what you do. And if you say that you and Pop had discussed this between yourselves, I believe you. But where I am in my life, $233,000 is a very big number. It's big enough that Jerry and I could drum up some options—maybe go back to school and dig ourselves out of this deepening financial hole."

## Endowment Effect

**The value we place on something is higher when we own it.** When we already possess something, we may place a higher value on surrendering it than we do when it is not already ours. If we choose to give it up, this choice involves a particular kind of loss. When this is our experience, we want the compensating benefits to be clear and substantial. When we ask or require stakeholders to give up something they already possess, they are likely to add value and weight to it. Effective decision-makers understand that people are reluctant to give up what they already have unless there is real benefit in doing so.

Unlike MaryAnn and Toby, John has worked hard to develop a business opportunity with his father. He is likely to place a greater value on it because of this owner relationship.

John: "The Williams Brothers offer is fair, and I can see how money now appeals to both of you. I see it differently because, in a sense, I think of myself as an owner, since I put so much into this joint venture with Pop. We had been meeting once a week for over a year, dreaming and scheming. With his blessing, I planned it and did a comprehensive financial analysis. I found the property we were going to use. I used $25,000 of my own money to option the property so Pop and I could work out the final details."

### Mental Accounting

**We keep different psychological accounts for valuing and comparing things.** People who spend hours driving to different stores to save $5 on groceries will jump at the chance to go on a vacation costing thousands because they account for it in different ways. We understand these different accounts only when we appreciate the different ways in which people compare and value. When someone's accounting system is different from ours, it is easy to dismiss his or her point of view as irrational or foolish. In order to learn about the unique ways in which people account for value, we must be willing to ask them and then listen.

> *The truth never arrives neatly wrapped.*
>
> **Thomas Powers**

Toby: "John, you're making a strong case about Pop's loyalty to his employees and what might happen to them if Williams Brothers takes over. Hey, all of us face uncertainties in life. My husband and I face uncertainties every day, and we're hoping to give our kids a leg up by giving them a good education—like you had. So I don't count the consequences to Pop's employees in my decision. That may sound cold, but it is just about dollars and cents for me. This decision strikes me as easier for you because you were working with Pop and you already have plenty of money. I have to take your word for it that your business plan is better for me, economically. And if it's not, I want to sell. It's that simple."

### Order/Recency Effect

**The order in which facts come to us affects the way we consider and weigh them.** One of our clients identified an unwritten norm in his organization that is consistent with this principle: *"The last loudest voice wins."* He describes the widespread perception that the person who weighs in last has disproportionate influence on the outcome. It matters who has the last word. It is also clear that being first matters. Initial statements, positions, and comments can set the tone and direction of all that follows. Negotiators know that the first meaningful offer on the table can establish the bargaining range for the offers that follow and thus shape the final solution.

> *The facts we see depend on where we are placed, and the habits of our eyes.*
>
> **Walter Lippmann**

It is easy for the mind to hold onto or become anchored to the first thing it encounters. A fact, an impression, or an opinion that comes to us first, or last, can have greater impact than information in between. The power of anchoring on the first perspective, or experiencing undue influence by the last, can be offset if we experiment with different perspectives and invite other people to offer alternative views.

In this case, the first number MaryAnn and Toby heard was the estate settlement amount, assuming the sale of the business. Given their financial circumstances, a large sum would likely command their attention.

> MaryAnn: "John, why don't you go over the ideas you and Pop were discussing when he died, especially the numbers about profit. As it stands, I can't seem to take my mind off the $233,000 I would get if we sell the business. That means $308,000 total. In my mind, that money is already in my bank account, and Jerry and I have quit our lousy jobs to go back to school. I find it hard to even think about turning down a sure thing like that."

## Judgmental Overconfidence

**We tend to overestimate the accuracy of our assumptions and predictions about future events.** An important reason we overestimate is that each of us has only part of the relevant information and we can't properly weigh the importance of what we don't know. Reducing our blind spots reduces overconfidence. When we consult only those who support our limited perceptions, we fool ourselves. A good decision-making process makes it safe for participants to ask pointed questions, test information, and uncover blind spots.

> *You know, Percy, everybody is ignorant, only on different subjects.*
> **Will Rogers**

John has lived and breathed real estate deals for twenty years. He has been very successful by any standard. Assume that John convinces the others to move forward with his plan. Will his comfort with the inherent risks and his justifiable confidence in his own judgment serve him and his sisters well?

> Phillip: "John, you have given this a lot of thought and already decided to invest time and money in the joint venture. To be fair to MaryAnn and Toby, who are just now hearing about all this, I hope you'll slow down and walk them through your thought process about both the risks and rewards of the joint venture. You have been honest in pointing out that there's no legal requirement that Gandalfo go forward with the joint venture. Given that, it seems only fair that we go over your financial analysis together and take a fresh look. You said that Gandalfo could anticipate $105,000 in profit from the new subdivision every year for five years. How did you come up with that number? How certain are you that MaryAnn and Toby will receive this payout? Would you be willing to consider taking your one-third as an owner of Gandalfo after they received their share? If you all decide not to sell, would you agree to buy them out if they become uncomfortable with the arrangement? That would decrease the risk for them and make your profit dependent on the accuracy of your judgment."

## Reactive Devaluation

Our evaluation of a proposal or idea can be different, depending on the source. When we are in an adversarial relationship, we may devalue an idea that we would regard more highly were it to come from a neutral party or a friend. In our work teams, families, and voluntary groups, we may be unable to give a proposal and its guiding values fair consideration when someone we dislike presents it. A good process can help separate the message from the messenger, allowing us to weigh the proposal more carefully.

> Toby: "John, everything you say may make perfect sense, but I can't help but think of all the times you ran things when we were growing up. You always made the plans and convinced us to do what **you wanted to do**. Sometimes your plans were good for me, and sometimes they weren't. I care about Pop's memory just as much as you do, but I'm not going to be sold on this idea just by your presentation. So forgive me if I take your predictions with a large grain of salt. And let's face it—the money just doesn't mean as much to you as it does to us. Frankly, you may have as much ego as assets tied up in this. Phillip, how can we assess John's idea to determine if it's really the best way to go?"

> *The house of delusions is cheap to build but drafty to live in.*
> **A. E. Houseman**

## Sunk Cost Fallacy

We tend to invest additional resources influenced more by what we have already expended than by the best use of the resources from now on. From failing companies to costly wars, continued investment of time, money, and energy in productive pursuits is often justified based on what has already been sunk into the project. Rather than asking the question, *"What is the best use of my time, money, and effort now?"* we spend even more trying to save or avoid losing what has already been spent. Instead of comparing future cost with future gain, we worry about what is past. Sometimes, this emphasis on salvaging past expenditures is rooted in the simple desire to avoid loss, as in the case of continuing life-support treatment in clearly futile cases. Other times, it is more about the psychological pain and loss of face that will come with the recognition of the loss.

> John: "Pop and I have already put $50,000 into the option on the property, $25,000 each. If we don't go forward with the joint venture, we lose this money. If we continue, it is applied to the purchase price. It may not mean much to you, but I have spent about one-quarter of my time for the last six months developing the business plan, and Pop has been lining up additional crews and subcontractors. We're ready to go! I am not willing to just write off all this time, effort, and money!"

### Status Quo Bias

**It is easier to leave things the same than choose to change.** We rest more comfortably in the known. There is a natural and powerful inertia to keep doing what you are doing. Considering change requires addressing uncertainties. This causes discomfort, so we come up with reasons to stay where we are. That said, sometimes it is helpful to con-

> *The only person that likes change is a wet baby.*
> **Roy Blitzer**

sider doing nothing as a formal option and analyze its value and consequences just as we evaluate our other choices.

In this case, the status quo is an operating family business. John has a plan to continue it and the expertise to carry it forward.

MaryAnn: "I don't know. I just don't know. I loved Pop, and I imagine that he would want the business to continue. Maybe I'm just feeling left out because I didn't have the overall picture. I do know that, besides us and the grandkids, the business was his life and the workers were like family. Selling out does seem like a radical step. I'm starting to think it might feel more comfortable to ride along for a while and see how it goes."

Toby: "We may never have a better chance to cash out than we have right now. I don't want to just ride along, MaryAnn. I want to think this through and make the best choice."

### Overload Factors

**We stop thinking clearly when we have too much to consider.** Information, choices, and numbers can overload us. Through our ability to "Google" almost anyone and anything, each of us has experienced the sensation of drowning in data without knowing more. We quickly reach a state of "analysis paralysis."

Although we think of choices as inherently desirable, more choices do not always produce greater satisfaction. If you have ever invited a three-year-old to choose among thirty-one flavors of ice cream, you know that having too many choices can impair our ability to make a decision. As a result, we may make no choice at all. Sometimes a simple, *"Vanilla or chocolate?"* works better.

Finally, faced with a decision requiring some math and number literacy, more than a few of us claim to suffer from math anxiety and number numbness. In their grip, we may fog over, freeze up, or act impulsively.

MaryAnn: "I feel so stupid. You've explained what you propose, and I don't know how to compare the numbers. I know my share of the Williams sale would be $233,000. But you said the profits would be $175,000 over five years. Why wouldn't I want more money now?"

## Denial

**We refuse to accept things as they truly are.** Why do we sometimes fail to see clearly? It may be our personal perspective or situation. It may be our actions' effect on others. It may be that we feel responsible or accountable. For example, instead of admitting that a decision has hurt others, we respond, *"It won't be so bad."* When looking at a situation that makes us uncomfortable, we make up a story so we don't have to deal with the truth. *"Uncle Walter isn't an alcoholic. He just likes to celebrate a lot."*

> *We don't know because we don't want to know.*
> **Aldous Huxley**

More than a few families and organizations hold an illusion of what psychologist Daniel Goleman calls "happy family." We overlook the imperfections and fault lines in our group and lift our eyes to an idealized picture of how we want to see ourselves and have others see us.

> Toby: "John, you have described three different ways that Pop would want to see the business continue. Pop never said a word to MaryAnn or me about it. He didn't leave a will providing for it. You say you've had conversations with him and invested money in this joint venture, but MaryAnn and I never heard about it. We've never had anything to do with the business, even as children when you worked on the construction crews. I don't buy this happy family scenario you are painting for us to be business partners. If Pop wanted this so much for all of us, why didn't he tell us? If you want to continue Gandalfo, why don't you make an offer to buy us out?"

## Rationalization

**We come up with explanations that make our decisions appear reasonable.** The more educated and intelligent we become, the more sophisticated is our ability to concoct rational cover stories for our actual motivations. Typically, these cover stories come in the form of an excuse, justification, or alibi. No matter the form, they are all counterfeit. There is only one real currency—our motivating value(s). Everything else is intellectual packaging.

> *Half the truth is often a great lie.*
> **Benjamin Franklin**

> John: "I wish the two of you could see that I want what is best for you. I am financially secure, and you could be too. Stick with me on this and five years from now, you will be grateful you did."

> Phillip: "Why don't you all go home and sleep on this. Let's meet tomorrow and see if you can reach a final decision. That gives me time to get back to the attorney for Williams Brothers by their deadline."

# Detours along the Road

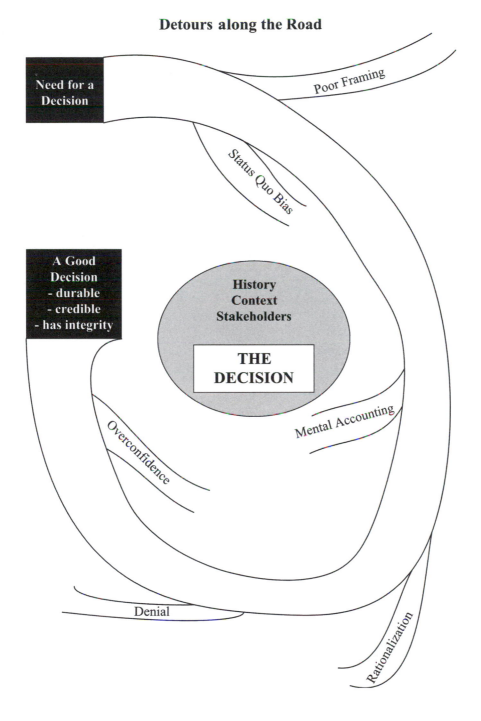

## WHAT YOU CAN DO: NAVIGATIONAL AIDS

The goal: Clarify understanding by steering clear of patterns of mental and emotional illusion.

### Give Intuition a Place at the Table

Intuition can be like a trusted friend who offers good advice. Intuition goes by many names: gut feeling, hunch, and sudden insight. To bring this source of advice into the conversation, you need to give voice to our intuitive sense. Use intuitive discomfort as information. The clash between intuition and analysis may indicate a need to develop more or better information. It may also be a warning signal to slow down and check out the situation more thoroughly.

- **Trust but verify.** Do not ignore your intuitive sense. Take it seriously but check it out. Look for supporting information that confirms what intuition is telling you.
- **Let your gut have its say.** Without censoring or editing, write down in a private place exactly what you feel in your gut. Once it is on paper, read it aloud. Ask yourself, *"Is this the sound of wisdom?"*
- **Pull up a chair.** Have a dialogue with your intuition by setting up two chairs. Sit in one and speak to your intuition. *"What is it you are trying to tell me?"* Move to the other chair and answer. If necessary, ask follow-up questions. *"But what about the impact on my wife's and my financial future if I take the new job?"*

**That evening over dinner at Toby's home . . .**

Toby: "Honey, where are you on this decision about Pop's estate?"

Jim: "I looked at all the papers and the offer from Williams Brothers. Tell me what you're thinking."

Toby: "In most ways, I lean toward accepting the offer. I trust John's knowledge and experience, and I do believe it's what Pop would want, for all the reasons John stated. But I have to tell you that I have a hunch it isn't a good thing for the family. I can't quite put my finger on it, but I am really uneasy."

Jim: "You usually have pretty good instincts. Remember that time I was hot to sell our house and move to a new, bigger place? I laid out all the reasons why it was a good idea. But you held your ground because of a hunch that it 'wasn't the right time.' Two weeks later, I got a better job offer, and we decided to move back to your hometown. So I'm inclined to go with your gut. Now, what future events might make your hunch right?"

### Make a Partial Commitment

When you lack the confidence to proceed yet must act, consider hedging your bets. Instead of making a final, irrevocable decision, make a partial commitment that offers you a chance to test and live with a decision.

- **Park by the side of the road.** Stay with your decision without acting on it. Just stop long enough to reflect and listen to your gut, your heart, and your internal messages about what you propose to do. For example, write your acceptance letter to a college or a new employer. Address the envelope. Put a stamp on it. Then leave it out on your kitchen table for twenty-four to forty-eight hours before you move forward. Let your feelings catch up with your decision.

- **Sleep on it.** Think of this as a brief stop by the side of the road—more like an overnight stay at a roadside campground. Second thoughts and deep misgivings are so common that many consumer laws have formalized the "right of rescission," a pause to test commitment. For a period of time after signing legal papers such as a home mortgage, the signer has a right to rescind or undo his commitment.

- **Make a trial announcement.** Create a private, safe opportunity to declare your proposed decision in front of witnesses who know you well. Make sure you notice everything about the way it sounds and feels to you. Ask your witnesses to give you feedback on how you come across as you deliver your decision.

    **A phone call between Toby and John.** Toby: "John, I need to ask you a favor. I'm close to a decision, but I'd like to visualize the reality of turning the offer down and co-owning Pop's business. Would you draw up a letter of agreement and address it to MaryAnn and me for our signatures? You understand this business, and you had already planned to do this with Pop. In your letter, cover money, decision-making, and anything else we need to be clear on if we go into business together. When I have it in front of me, I will sit with it for twenty-four hours to better imagine what it means to turn down Williams Brothers."

### Step Back and Take a Look

It helps to get the problem out of our heads and hearts and hold it out in front of us, so we can check it out. We can balance our subjectivity, slow down, and get a better look if we represent the problem or the decision in writing.

- **Do the math.** Use a spreadsheet or a piece of paper. Get the numbers that are important on paper and work with them directly. If you are unsure about how to do this, then find someone (friend, accountant, financial advisor) who can help make sense of the numbers.

- **Make a balance sheet.** Use the "Balance Sheet" form in the Appendix to do a plus/minus evaluation of the decision. What matters to you becomes the key criterion for assessing positive and negative aspects of a proposed option.

- **Post it on the wall.** To get more distance, take a big piece of paper (flip chart, poster board, butcher paper) and write down your options in big letters. Highlight your values that link to each option. Tape this up on a wall so you can move around, look at it, and consider it.

**A sheet taped to the refrigerator in MaryAnn's kitchen.**

---

### Option 1 take Williams Brothers deal

- Get larger sum of money now ... $233,000 (FREEDOM TO DO WHAT WE WANT)
- No uncertainties about operation of business and the future (PEACE OF MIND)
- ???

### Option 2 co-own Gandalfo with John and Toby

- Get some money now ... $75,000 (SOME FREEDOM)
- Likely to get a steady stream of income for five years ... $175,000 (ECONOMIC SECURITY, STABILITY)
- Uncertainties about the business, potential hassles with John (STRESS)
- Potential for bigger payoff down the road as business maintains or increases its value (ECONOMIC SECURITY)
- Honoring Pop's legacy and doing what he would probably want (RESPECT, FAMILY)

---

### Flip the Frame

Consciously change the way you view the issue by framing it in different ways. Specifically, change terms to state the issue first positively, then negatively. Look for important reference points. Next, increase or decrease the prominence of the reference point in the statement to see how this influences your response to the decision.

Change the frame:

- from positive to negative or negative to positive
- from narrow to broad or broad to narrow
- from gain to loss or loss to gain.

John: "MaryAnn, I understand you're looking at the immediate gain of $233,000 if we accept the Williams Brothers offer. I'm asking that you consider what you may be losing. First, there is the opportunity to build economic security by owning a share of a very strong, profitable business. Don't forget that some very sharp business people are willing to pay a lot of money for this company. Second, you are giving up a chance to honor Pop and his work by carrying it on as a family business. This could be a place where your daughter could work summers and learn about work and money. Finally, you are not showing Pop's employees the consideration Pop would want you to. Don't you think that's the right think to do?"

### Find Some Fresh Eyes

The tougher the issue and the more isolated we are, the easier it is to fall into common traps. Formally or informally, bring in a thoughtful person or persons who can look at the decision without your baggage. In a personal situation, this might be a professional such as a lawyer, therapist, financial advisor, or accountant. It might also be a trusted relative, good friend, or neighbor. In an organization, an ombudsman or trustworthy colleague could fill the bill.

- **Make the case by laying out the facts.** Think of yourself as an advocate trying to make the factual case for what you are inclined to do. The other person can play the role of sounding board, asking you questions and reflecting back what she hears from you.
- **Share your doubts and concerns.** Be honest about your misgivings with your advisor, and ask her to give you a reality check.
- **Appoint someone as a critical evaluator.** Authorize someone to play a strong, even aggressive role in questioning your proposed decision and the clarity of your reasoning.

   **A call between MaryAnn and Jane, a friend and mentor.** MaryAnn: "Thanks for making time for me. I have an important decision to make in the next couple of days about my father's estate. I value your judgment. If I lay out what I am thinking and what I plan to do, will you ask me tough questions that challenge the logic of my plan?"

### Make Your Values Loyal Allies

Outdoor educators teach children to "hug a tree" when they become disoriented in the woods. This simple reminder, which any child can remember, has an analog for adults facing tough choices. *"Hug your values— hold them close."* When we keep these important principles close, they provide a solid, reassuring presence. This quiets us down, keeps us from overreacting, and prevents us from straying away into thickets of facts and feelings.

- **Post your values on the wall.** Many organizations have ethics codes or statements of core values framed on the wall. Yet these formal displays usually fade into the background. Just write down what matters to you in large letters on a flip chart, butcher paper, or poster board. Ask yourself where those principles lead you as you move toward your decision.

- **Say your values aloud.** The spoken word has meaning. Try speaking what matters to feel yourself lean into what is most important.
- **Be a judge.** Ask an ally to advocate for your values so you can step into the role of a judge, listening to someone else argue for what is most important to you in this decision.

## The Final Decision. . .

John: "I still want to stay in the business together and move forward with the development plan."

Toby: "Jim and I talked it through. My instincts are somewhat negative, but we will go along if MaryAnn does. That way it would be a family decision. If MaryAnn doesn't want to do it, then that tips me over to wanting the buy out."

MaryAnn: "This has been really stressful for me. I'd like to be able to say yes, but my family and financial situation make it crystal clear that I should cash out and get my life in order. John, I believe in you. I just need to focus on my life, not on being co-owner of a construction business. I hope you understand."

After a long, poignant silence, Phillip spoke. "John, I have an idea. Since you are already one-third owner of the business, is there any way you could buy out MaryAnn and Toby and move ahead with the plans you made with your father?"

John: "I'll need some time to think about it and talk to my banker."

## Later that day. . .

John: "Here is what I propose. I'll match the Williams Brothers offer so each of you will receive a total of $233,000 in value as follows:

- a down payment of $133,000 in cash within thirty days
- a promissory note for $30,000 carrying interest at 4 percent, payable monthly for five years
- a $70,000 investment in the business, for which you will each hold 10 percent of the stock in Gandalfo. I will make your profits a priority and agree not to take any money out for myself until each of you receives your 10 percent share.

This will give me the flexibility to move ahead while providing you with most of the money now and reducing the risk to you. It means a lot to me to consider this a family business, and I hope this addresses your reluctance. At the end of five years, if you want to stay in the business, you can choose to do so, or I will buy you out for $70,000 plus 4 percent interest or fair market value, whichever is greater. That way, you won't be trapped in the business as a minority shareholder. What do you say?"

MaryAnn: "I am touched by how hard you are trying to make this work. With the money you are offering up front, I think James and I can move forward. Toby, are you still willing to go along with me on this and stay in?"

Toby: "Absolutely. John, we're counting on you. Uncle Phil, can you draw up a good agreement that captures John's offer?"

# 7

## Bridge the Cultural Divide

*Every reporter is a citizen of somewhere and a believer in something.*
James Tobin

We first sight difficult choices through unique frames and angles. Where do these different perspectives come from? The answer is culture. If a multistory building shapes our perspectives, then culture is its blueprint. Culture tells us where to stand, it frames the windows, and it defines our first glimpse of the courtyard. Culture choreographs appropriate ways of being and behaving and teaches us how to navigate our world. We follow its rules about personal space and our place in the natural world, about our own identities and where we fit in with others, and about what we may or may not say. Each of us belongs to more than one cultural group at any given time, be it family, faith, society, profession, neighborhood, or nation. Each of us is a living, breathing, multicultural microcosm, for whom a single blueprint is insufficient.

Previous chapters describe the importance of understanding context when making decisions. History, personal experience, roles, and relationships all influence what matters to us, whether or not we know it. This chapter singles out one aspect of context for careful consideration. When we fail to attend to the dimension of culture during the decision-making process, we create serious obstacles.

> *It is not our differences that divide us; rather it is our inability to recognize, address and celebrate those differences.*
> **Audre Lord**

## A TALE OF TWO FAMILIES

Caroline Tafoya and Dan White are second-year pediatric residents at University Hospital. They have been through medical school and internship together and are close friends. Over the years, they have traded insights, advice, and large doses of moral support.

Lately they have been engaged in an ongoing discussion concerning Baby Marie, a nine-month-old who has been in a coma since birth. "It's so hard," said Caroline, "to see that tiny infant—day after day—connected to tubes with no hope of recovery." Last Tuesday was an especially difficult day, Caroline told Dan over coffee in the hospital cafeteria. "The family arrived for one of their periodic visits—and by family I mean friends, relatives, you name it. They 'camp out' in the waiting room for a couple of days, as Dr. Walsh puts it, then disappear for weeks at a time.

"I feel sorry for them. I know they come a long way, and I don't think they fully understand Marie's condition. This time I tried talking to them again. The uncle speaks for the parents and family, and he always says the same thing. 'Do anything and everything you can for Marie. When it's time for God to take her, he will.' No one in the family will permit me to talk about the prospect of Marie's death."

"It's tough," agreed Dan. "Why don't the docs deal with the parents directly? That's state law—they should be Marie's decision-makers. Has anyone talked about going to court to end this futile care?"

He paused. "Well, I've got my own story. Remember Johnny Grant, the little Deaf boy? And how we'd proposed a cochlear implant to help him hear? Well, his mother, who is also Deaf, now refuses to consent to the procedure. Get this— she says, 'I'm Deaf, his father's Deaf, and Johnny will be better off growing up Deaf. That's our culture.' Of course, I can't speak directly to them. It's all done through whatever interpreter the hospital can provide. When I looked at the father in disbelief, he shrugged and looked away, as though he didn't want to rock the boat with his wife. We're considering getting a court order."

As the two friends rose to leave, Dan gave Caroline a hug and added, "Hey, good luck tomorrow. Don't you have your performance evaluation coming up?"

## CULTURE

References to culture are everywhere. It's hard to read a newspaper or open a magazine without encountering stories about cultural conflicts, whether it's Muslims and Christians or cruisers and law enforcement. Culture is a concept most people recognize. When different groups must understand each other and work together, a shallow understanding of cultural differences jeopardizes their ability to make good decisions. Even when participants appear to share similar cultural backgrounds and values, unseen or unacknowledged differences can negatively affect the process.

Culture is a relatively new term in the English language, although its roots trace back to Latin and Old French words meaning "to till the soil."

## Building a Bridge

Current usage adds "social blueprint" to the definition of culture as a cultivated medium for improved growth. Each of us grows into who and what our culture(s) intends.

Cultural makeup is more than our census bureau classification. This chapter challenges two perspectives that shape our idea of culture. The first perspective limits culture to ethnicity or country of origin. While tribal and national origins prescribe certain behaviors, so do our families, professions, faith communities, work environments, and social/political affiliations. Sometimes those blueprints and plans for us agree. Sometimes they don't. When there is conflict, we need to resolve it.

The second perspective rations culture, only one to a person. Because of our concurrent membership in multiple groups, each of us is a unique, multicultural phenomenon. When we know ourselves as diverse and cross-cultural persons, it is easier to appreciate differences in others.

To overcome these limited perspectives, it is important to unravel our own cultural complexity before labeling others. Understanding our own cultures before starting to work with others to bridge cultural differences smoothes the road to a good decision.

The following week Dan asked Caroline how her evaluation with her department chair had gone.

"It went well," Caroline answered, "but it's always been the hardest thing I have to do, to brag about myself. I'd rather just do the best job I can and be recognized for my efforts. I don't need to stand out. That's the way I was raised." She smiled and added, "Well, I should tell you that I did something else that was hard for me. I challenged Dr. Walsh when I heard he'd told Baby Marie's family that they should visit more often. He told them to find some place else to stay when they come and, from now on, it would be the parents, and only the parents, with whom he'd discuss treatment decisions. I understand his desire to deal with the parents—but I swear he didn't even have a clue as to which ones they were. He's been overseeing Marie's treatment all this time, and he doesn't realize how far the family has to travel, their financial constraints, the uncle's role in the family, or anything else for that matter. I told Dr. Walsh I wished he would treat them more respectfully, even sit down and listen to them—then maybe he'd see some positive results. He reminded me that he'd been practicing medicine since before I could drive. Then he kind of harrumphed and said he'd think about it. So how was your week?"

"Not much better," said Dan. "I confronted Johnny's mother. I told her what I truly believe is in Johnny's best medical interests—that it just didn't make sense to withhold medical treatment when he could in fact be helped. She wouldn't budge, so I persuaded the hospital attorney to petition the court for temporary guardianship of Johnny, so we could perform the surgery. It's what Johnny needs, regardless of what his family says. Can you believe it? The judge refused and sent it back to us. 'Try to work this out among yourselves, as parents and doctors. It will be much better if you can come up with a solution you agree on instead of a judicial decree that will only harden the conflict.' He even suggested that I speak to members of the Cochlear Implant Center as well as representatives of our local Deaf community.

> Lamadrid defined negotiating identity as using social or cultural signals. . .He likened it to a train using a railroad switch to alternate between parallel tracks. The train is still the same train though it switches tracks from time to time.
>
> **Aurelio Sanchez**

I was disappointed, to say the least. Then, to make matters worse, my department chair told me to meet with Johnny's family—again—and try to negotiate a solution acceptable to all of us. First, I don't think that's possible. Second, I don't have the time. Third, it feels like passing the buck or, worse, seriously compromising Johnny's health. Somebody is going to go away angry."

What don't we know about the back story here? What are Caroline and Dan's stories? Who are Baby Marie's family members? Where do they come from, and what matters to them? What does Johnny's mother mean by Deaf culture?

Caroline Tafoya understood Baby Marie's family because she also grew up on the reservation in a traditional Navajo family. She made her decision to enter medical school following lengthy talks with family, friends, and a medicine man. In many ways, hers was a community decision.

Dan White appreciated swift action and efficient problem solving. He grew up in New York City and was the third generation among the men in his family to become either physicians or lawyers. Caroline and Dan joked that they were indeed an odd couple, even though their respect for one another began early in their relationship. They were paired together during the gross anatomy lab their first year at medical school. Dan remembered watching Caroline pause at the door to the dissection room and wait. At first he thought she was squeamish. Then he realized something else was going on. Later that year, Caroline persuaded faculty to design a ritual of respect for the moment when medical students met "their" cadaver. She discovered she was not alone in her desire to honor what would be a yearlong relationship with a body, a body that had until recently been a person.

> *When becoming physicians, young medical students undergo dramatic personal transformations, often in a relatively short time, that renders them unrecognizable to themselves.*
> **Rita Charon**

When the first-year medical students wrote commitment statements about medicine, Dan's oath caught Caroline's attention. In it, she heard the voice of an Anglo man for whom the medical profession was clearly a calling, not a lucrative career move. When he chose pediatrics, he did so to the dismay of his father and grandfather. To this day, their words echo in Dan's mind. "Pediatrics just doesn't carry the prestige that other subspecialties do. Why settle for a place so far down on the medical food chain? Not to mention the paltry pay."

Culture imposes a system of rules that prescribe such behaviors as:

- manners and etiquette
- life-and-death rituals
- the language we use
- how we deal with conflict
- what career path we choose
- what constitutes appropriate behavior at work and at home.

> *Culture is fundamentally a property of information, a grammar for organizing reality, for imparting meaning to the world.*
> **Raymond Cohen**

These rules create a group's identity and govern its behavior, just as grammar generates a unified language.

Many members of the signing Deaf community assert that they are indeed a culture. As a group, they share common methods of communicating, they have their own language, and they interact with their world in common ways, that is, visually. Their cultural perspective is different from the medical or pathological view, which treats deafness as an illness or dysfunction to cure or fix and assigns to Deaf people the role of patient or disabled person. These two views of the same courtyard are strikingly different, although not always mutually exclusive.

Family, profession, business, and geography give us language and social structure and teach us what to believe. Each affiliation thrives on a shared memory and set of experiences that the others may not be able to access. When multiple affiliations converge in us, they can create conflict. Then, our role with ourselves and with others becomes ambassadorial. We negotiate among our personal cultures, although it's not immediately obvious which voice will prevail at any given time.

A physician colleague tells the following story. She is the medical director for a large nursing home with a university affiliation. Many of her patients are research subjects in studies on aging and the elderly. She helped design one study that involved videotaping residents as they discussed what was important to them in doctor–patient relations. While she values geriatric research, she takes great care to insure that participating residents have given fully informed consent. When she heard that a certain patient of hers had just given consent to participate in this study, she was surprised and worried.

> *If we cannot end our differences, at least we can help make the world safe for diversity.*
> **John Fitzgerald Kennedy**

"My colleagues sometimes ask me how I, as an African-American physician from an urban university, came to be so close to this patient, an elderly white woman from Appalachia. I remind them that I'm originally from rural Alabama, and what this woman and I see in each other is not black and white, city and country. It's the South that connects us, which is why I went to see her about the research study."

"You're right, doctor, I didn't want someone asking me all those questions in front of a camera. It's none of their business. But I thought it would be rude to say no. Besides, I heard that you were involved in the project, and I thought if I refused, you wouldn't be my doctor anymore. So I said yes."

"As Southern women, she and I value our privacy. We also value civility and graciousness. I explained to her that I would still be her doctor and that she should express what she really did or did not want to do."

"I'd rather not participate."

"And so she didn't."

> *What we have to do. . .is to find a way to celebrate our diversity and debate our differences without fracturing our communities.*
> **Hillary Rodham Clinton**

The world is a small place. Because of our interdependence, communicating across difference is more important than ever. Whether the issue is personal, religious, professional, or intergovernmental, barricading ourselves against those different from us simply does not work. By now, most of us are weary of the so-called "culture wars," where combatants hurl values at each other, settling only for total victory and domination of an adversary. Our first truce should be with ourselves when competing cultural voices demand our allegiance and brook no compromise. When we make peace with ourselves, we're more likely to do so with others. *"First I must reconcile my own Navajo roots with Western medicine, my respect for traditional healers with an appreciation for medical science."*

Culture gives us a sense of identity, hierarchy, and belonging, along with distinct attitudes toward time and space. Because we belong to more than one cultural group, we often need to calibrate our orientation. You don't have to be an anthropologist or social scientist to do this. This chapter highlights three quite ordinary dimensions of culture that apply to everyone:

- **Personal identity**: Where do we find it?
- **Relationships**: How do we interact with others in our lives?
- **Our place in the world**: How do we use time, space, and language to orient ourselves and fit in?

When we manage these cultural dimensions skillfully, we create the environment for good decision-making.

## IDENTITY: WHO ARE YOU?

Cultural competence starts at home. We can improve our decision-making skills if we ask questions of ourselves and work out the answers before labeling others. When we've reconciled our own tangled roots, we are more likely to make space for others' differences and dissonance.

Our identity depends on biology. It also comes from a cultural heritage we acquire socially, not genetically. Societies and groups create and transmit their complex and multilayered cultures to individuals. We inherit much of our identity in this way.

Consider Caroline and Dan. Caroline is Navajo, a physician, a student, a woman with traditional and rural roots. Dan is Anglo, a physician, a product of urban life, the son and grandson of men for whom professional identity carries weight and prestige.

> *Contextual objectivity: A view from nowhere.*
> **Arthur Kleinman**

Even though each of us has an equally complex and unique pedigree, we rarely take stock of ourselves in this way.

Two contrasting views about identity influence our approach to decision-making. The first view has to do with where we locate our identity: inside ourselves or in the group. We may define ourselves first and fundamentally as unique individuals, or our identity may come from membership in a group or community. Ask yourself the following questions: How do you introduce yourself to others? After your name, do you start with where you live and what you do for a living? *"I'm from Chicago and I sell insurance."* Or do you first acknowledge your ancestors and family, faith, or nationality? *"My family originally comes from the Scottish Highlands." "I am a Buddhist." "I am from Mexico."*

The second view flows from the first and speaks to our sense of purpose and fulfillment. Some people value personal achievement and advancement as well as individual assertiveness. Others concentrate on building healthy relationships and sustaining a high quality of life for their community.

> *Father Latour judged that, just as it was the white man's way to assert himself in any landscape, to change it, make it over a little. . .it was the Indian's way to pass through a country without disturbing anything; to pass and leave no trace, like fish through the water, or birds through the air. It was the Indian manner to vanish into the landscape, not to stand out against it.*
>
> **Willa Cather**

Neither perspective is right or wrong, just powerful. Nor are these ways of establishing identity mutually exclusive. Many of us have some of each. However, they do lead us in different directions and can cause confusion and conflict, both in our own lives as well as with others. As a child, Caroline defined herself first as a member of her clan and her community. She learned that people, like houses, should blend in. Whether in architecture or individual performance, standing apart from others is rude. *"Promoting myself, for purposes of professional advancement, is the hardest thing I have to do."*

Professional medical culture taught her something else. At least in the United States, the focus is on individual professionals and their autonomous practices. As she had heard Dan say, on more than one occasion, *"I'm well trained, and ultimately it is my responsibility to determine the best treatment for my patients."* From this perspective, personal achievement, excellence, rights, responsibilities, and health belong to individuals, not groups. *"How can it be right for a group, especially one that calls itself the Deaf culture, to impose its will on an individual child who has his own health needs? What business is it of theirs?"* This view of identity is intensely individual.

Dan's early experiences prepared him for this highly individualistic profession. However, his notion of health as maximizing an individual's ability to function did not prepare him to understand, much less accept, the idea or legitimacy of a Deaf culture. Nor was he looking forward to spending precious time listening to everyone, once again, when he faced so many other urgent decisions. He solved problems by deciding firmly and with dispatch. *"What is there to know about the issue*

> *No culture can live, if it attempts to be exclusive.*
> **Mohandas Gandhi**

*that I don't already know? I know the right treatment, I know what is right for Johnny, and, after all, it's Johnny, not his mother, who is my patient, isn't it?"*

## RELATIONSHIPS: HOW DO YOU POSITION YOURSELF WITH OTHERS?

In our work environment, we may refer to those above and below us. We all have people we look up to and those who, by virtue of their positions, hand down decisions. *"Why don't you take Baby Marie's family to court and ask a judge to hand down a decision?"* Many parents describe their approach to child rearing and discipline as vertical, from the parent down to the child: *"Because I'm the Mommy."* One way in which we orient ourselves to others is through vertical relationships. In some societies, for example in caste systems, there is no movement up or down between levels. Where you're born is where you remain. In other societies, movement up and down is possible and depends on certain prescribed behaviors and attributes,

> *Suppose we were able to share meanings freely without a compulsive urge to impose our view or conform to those of others and without distortion and self-deception. Would this not constitute a real revolution in culture?*
>
> **David Bohm**

such as work, wealth, and education. In either case, such relationships among people are vertical. We look up or we look down.

At other times, we look sideways and across the table. People who teach adults know that a top–down approach to learning frequently fails. In the United States, physician–patient relationships have evolved from something akin to a parent–child relationship into more of a partnership. *"If the patient isn't firmly on board, my job is much harder. We each bring important information and perspective to the treatment plan."*

Some authors and business consultants tout the benefits of horizontal relationships in the workplace, where employees organize according to roles, skills, and abilities. Everyone and every role are necessary for an organization's successful functioning. Both productivity and employee morale improve in a more collaborative, less competitive environment, where interdependence trumps independence. For example, W. L. Gore and Associates shuns titles, special offices, and levels of management. Their record of innovation and their commitment to horizontal relationships contribute to their consistent ranking as one of the best American companies to work for.

*"I have suggested to the board that we include staff at our annual board/management retreat, to help us brainstorm our agency's direction and agenda for the coming year."*

Supporters of flattening the hierarchy point to increased accountability as well as less buck passing and learned helplessness. Authority and responsibility reside in the same person, regardless of her position in the organizational flow chart. While extra layers might improve a wedding cake, they can impede a business' smooth functioning.

Often, people bring a personal bias in favor of vertical or horizontal ways of organizing relationships, no matter the situation or their role. For example, some believe that women and men, clergy and the laity, top management and staff, teachers and students, parents and children, all benefit from relationships that are as collaborative and horizontal as possible and appropriate. Others feel more comfortable in groups where authority and the chain of command are clear and where they understand their place and role. They know where they stand.

Others shift easily between different hierarchical expectations, depending on the situation. Your experience at church may be quite traditional and vertically arranged, while problem solving within your family is highly collaborative. You may work for a company where lines between management and staff are blurred, yet on weekends when you serve in the Air Force Reserve, you know who gives and who follows orders.

When we face tough choices that involve others, we all bring our own experience of relationships to the table. It is important to know and communicate our expectations and to invite others to do the same.

Knowing how we fit in with others answers a number of questions:

- Whose decision is this?
- Is there a degree of comfort with shared decision-making or a preference for efficiency and clarity that comes with a single decision-maker?
- How do different groups designate decision-makers? In Baby Marie's family, the uncle speaks for the family. According to U.S. law, the parents decide on behalf of a child or the patient on behalf of himself. In other groups, an extended community may weigh in, as with Caroline's career decision.
- What commitments do different relationships bring? What agendas do roles impose?

When a group comes to a decision-making table, who speaks first, or at all? The person who speaks first often sets the framework and terms of the discussion. In medical settings, it is common for physicians to present the medical issues first. *"Let's be clear about the medical facts. Johnny is Deaf, and we have a surgical procedure that can fix that. He is at the perfect age for such a procedure to succeed. It's as simple as that."* If the relationships are vertical, the person with the most power usually goes first. If the relationships are horizontal, the person directing the conversation may ask, *"Who would like to start?"*

Some participants expect debate, while others prefer dialogue. *"Try to work this out among yourselves."* There may be an assumption of a win/lose outcome. *"I know someone is going to walk away angry."* It may be important but unstated that everyone should agree. These are important issues. Clarity about these different views of relationship helps develop a good interaction.

The first step is to see the differences. The second is to respect them. The third is to manage them.

## THE WORLD: HOW DO YOU FIT IN?

**Time, space,** and **place** play important roles in decision-making. *"I don't have time to spend on endless negotiation and discussion. The family disappears for weeks on end. When they come back, they camp out in the hospital. There are too many of them, and they crowd us. Can't they find a motel?"* Effective decision-makers take time to uncover the different expectations of time and place that people bring to the table.

Besides showing us how to navigate time and space, culture also guides the use of **language** in specific situations. *"They won't talk about death. Baby Marie will die, but we can't get them to talk about that. They just speak about God's will. That doesn't solve the medical problem."* Let's look at several features of time, space and place, and language that affect the decision-making process.

People experience time differently. It may be a commodity that we spend, jealously guard, sometimes waste, or never have enough of. *"I don't have time to waste on endless discussion when so many other decisions and people need my attention."* Or it simply may surround us, wherever we are, doing what we need to do, never too short, never too long, always just what it is. *"They stay away for weeks, then reappear and stay for days on end. It's as if they have no sense of time and the inconvenience they're causing."* Again, neither approach to time is right or wrong. It is the failure to understand how people live in and with time that can derail an otherwise healthy decision-making process. *"If you don't have time to do it right the first time, when will you have time to fix it when it falls apart?"*

People have different preferences and needs with respect to personal space. We know how close we like to be when speaking to someone and the point where a stranger's presence begins to intrude into our personal space. In meetings, there are room arrangements we prefer and places we like to sit. How we arrange the room and how we place chairs at a table send a message. *"Whenever Dr. Walsh meets with Baby Marie's family, he sits at the head of the table. Sometimes there aren't enough chairs for all the family. He doesn't seem to understand the effect that has on this family."*

Cultures understand place and space differently. For example, some of us believe in ownership, or at least proprietorship, of buildings and land.

*"I've finally earned myself a corner office on the top floor." "It's important to us, as parents, that our children own their own home. If necessary, we'll help them."*

Others believe we belong and should be welcome wherever we go. *"They treat the hospital like their personal living space. There isn't room for all of them here, in our hospital, while we're trying to take care of patients." "When we come to visit, we don't feel like we belong. We're treated like unwelcome guests."*

All cultures prescribe what their members may and may not talk about, and with whom. *"I understand why the family won't talk about the fact that Baby Marie is certainly going to die. I understand them. I, too, learned not to talk about death directly, lest I unwittingly hasten its arrival."* Some subjects are permitted, others are taboo. *"It's not that we don't accept death. It's that we believe death comes in its own time, not ours. I also learned deep respect for a dead body. Facing a year in the gross anatomy lab with 'my' cadaver profoundly challenged my beliefs. I needed to confront my feelings and memorialize an important relationship. It turned out to be important for non-Indian students as well."* There are rules for how we address each other. *"I learned to respect my elders and not talk back to them. When I confronted my attending physician about what he said to Baby Marie's family, I felt as though I had broken a basic rule. But then, so did he, when he spoke to them that way."*

Language has many purposes, such as:

- sharing information
- staking out territory
- asserting expertise
- gaining superiority
- establishing or sustaining relationships
- recording history
- transmitting culture.

Different cultures, different groups, and different people use language to achieve different ends, depending on the situation. Effective decision-makers are willing to learn why, and how, they and others converse.

Everyone speaks several languages, by which we mean something more than fluency in English, Spanish, or Farsi. Each of us internalizes our family's dialect, our profession's vocabulary, our friends' and communities' communication habits, our nation's way of speaking to the world. You should assume that, around a large decision-making table, people are speaking different languages, even if they sound the same. Effective decision-makers are multilingual. They take time to explain themselves, find the right language for the situation, and understand and interpret what others are really saying.

> Over coffee, a Navajo social worker observed to Dan and Caroline, "In my experience, white people talk too much. Informed consent, living wills, advance directives, and professional conferences are good examples. People think that if they can find the right words for a situation—the more words the better—then understanding will increase. I encourage them to listen to the silence."

## WHAT YOU CAN DO

### *Know Yourself*

The goal: Manage your own multicultural reality before tackling someone else's.

There are steps you can take to anticipate and navigate cultural influences during the decision-making process. Start with the following suggestions and questions about your own culture. Then, when it is important for you to know, invite others to describe theirs. By doing so, you may avoid and remove potentially disastrous obstacles along the way.

### Take a Cultural Inventory

Describe the groups to which you belong. Start a list of their rules:

- **Family:** *"My family thinks of itself as middle class—British and German-American extraction. We tend to be private when it comes to money matters, and we keep conflicts and differences to ourselves."*
- **Profession or business:** *"I teach philosophy to adults, and I've learned that these students are highly motivated, don't want to be treated like children, learn best experientially, and want to know why I teach and test the way I do."*
- **Faith community:** *"I come from a long line of Presbyterians who are highly independent and individualistic and expect people to assume responsibility for themselves; our lives and faith are interwoven with a strong sense of social justice."*
- **Gender:** *"As a woman, I tend to prefer collaboration over competition in the workplace."*
- **Geographic region:** *"I come from Southern California, where people seem more relaxed and open with strangers."*
- **Nationality:** *"My family comes from Central America. Our parents encouraged us to take an interest in politics and current events. Conversation around the dinner table was always lively, although not necessarily good for digestion."*

When you introduce yourself to others, which of the above groups do you mention, and in what order? *"I am an economist working for the Canadian government, although I come from Ireland." "I was born and raised in Jerusalem, am the mother of two sons who have dual citizenship—Israel and the United States—and am a postdoctoral fellow at the NIH."*

Describe the social blueprint, the expectations, that each group imposes on you and the identity conflicts. *"I'm an Irish-Catholic, oldest of four sons, about to marry a divorced Israeli woman with two children."* Where is there agreement or at least no open conflict? *"It's hard for our parents. They love us and see how much we care for each other. They're doing the best they can."*

When you've completed your personal inventory, reflect on the person you see. Does this vary according to the situation or context? If you can, draw a picture or diagram of your own multicultural tapestry. When you bring this inventory to the decision-making table, use your cultural self-awareness to improve your understanding of others.

### Explore Your Relationships

Pick two or three of the most important groups to which you belong and describe their rules for engaging others. *"I'm second generation Italian, the mother of four, and mayor of our community. I believe in airing our differences, whether in my family or on the city council. Strong feelings and loud voices don't intimidate me. Everyone needs to be involved and speak up." "I am the executive director of Health Care for the Homeless. My professional background is in psychology and social work. I grew up in rural New Hampshire, where we kept to ourselves and didn't talk much. To this day, I relate best to people of action and few words."*

After you've selected your group affiliations, answer the following questions about relationships:

- Does the group favor vertical or horizontal relationships? *"As a Muslim woman, when I travel to my family's village, I understand that women have a defined role and I am expected to marry the man they choose for me."*
- Does your personal comfort zone align more with vertical or horizontal relationships? *"My family comes from a traditional village, but we have lived in the United States for years. Although I understand the importance of family tradition, I generally prefer horizontal relationships in families and between women and men."*
- When you make decisions, what kinds of interactions with others do you find most productive, or does this vary from situation to situation? *"I appreciate leaders who understand that decisions made too quickly often*

*cost us dearly in time, money, and loss of credibility. Good leaders find time to involve others, listen well, and avoid hasty decisions."*

- What relationships and interactions make you uncomfortable in decision-making settings? *"I dread meetings with no clear-cut agenda and no apparent direction. I want to know what the task is, what information is available, and I like to move swiftly and efficiently toward a decision."*

- Do you prefer competition or collaboration? *"I learn a great deal when people debate opposing positions and challenge each other's assumptions."*

- Do you prefer to speak or listen? *"I sometimes forget how little I learn when I'm the one who is talking."*

### Orient Yourself

Time, space, and language play different roles in different cultures. Understanding yours and others' approaches to time will help you avoid some easily preventable conflicts during a decision-making process.

Start with yourself, and think about **time.**

- Some people equate time with clock time and organize their day accordingly. *"I start my day at five thirty in the morning with a run, followed by breakfast. I'm at work by seven thirty. I always take an hour for lunch, pick up my daughter at day care at six, and make sure I have at least two hours to spend with her and her father before she goes to bed. I wish I had more time."*

- Others think of time as a vessel to be filled and lived, a constantly renewing resource. *"I prefer to spend as much time with patients as they need, regardless of the clock. Of course, the HMO I work for has a different approach." "Don't just do something. Stand there."*

- You may experience time as linear. If you do, the past is gone forever; you are always moving into and toward the future. *"I exercise and eat a healthy diet, so that twenty years from now I'll still be able to do the things I enjoy." "As you sow, so shall you reap." "It's important to apply lessons learned in the past to future situations."*

- Or you may live in the present rather than dwell in the past or anticipate the future. *"I exercise, eat well, and enjoy life, one day at a time." "Today, this moment is all we ever have. Live it fully." "Pay attention to what is in front of your nose." "Be mindful."*

- You may also experience time as cyclical, best understood in terms of recurring patterns, such as the seasons, the life cycles of plants, animals, and humans, or the phases of the moon. *"The other day, I remembered my mother as I was looking at my adult daughter. I thought: What goes around comes around." "I am on my third CEO in ten years. I've learned what to expect. Some things never change."*

- You may think of time as a commodity that you save and spend. *"I never have enough time. I try not to waste time on unimportant tasks." "It is important that I and others be punctual and that we not overstay our welcome. I value efficiency. I worry that people who multitask don't do any one thing well."*

Next, think about what **place** and **space** mean to you. If a decision involves property or place, don't assume that you know what these mean for all the participants. Find out. How you organize the decision-making space, both figuratively and literally, can affect the outcome.

- Place for you may be where you are currently standing. *"Wherever I am at any given time is home."*
- It may be where you come from. *"I grew up on the Pacific Ocean and will always have salt water in my blood."*
- Cultures relate to land in different ways. Some believe that people can and should own land. Others believe that all places belong to everyone, or no one. Is ownership of property fundamental to your worldview? *"I believe people have a right to protect their own land and home. After all, it's theirs." "No one can own what is not theirs. We are guests on this planet and should always behave as respectful visitors."*
- Cultures also define appropriate personal space. Different groups and different people have their own comfort zones. When you are in a group, how close is too close? *"I don't like it when people get in my face." "I grew up in Japan, and I'm used to people living and working in tight, crowded spaces."*

Finally, think about **language**. Effective decision-makers are accomplished linguists. They detect how others use language and adjust the dialogue accordingly. Their goal is mutual understanding and transparency.

- What languages (in the usual sense) do you speak or understand? Think of ways in which different languages present or describe the world. In Turkish, there is a separate verb tense for having witnessed an event: *"He went to the store"* in this tense means that I actually saw him go. In French and Spanish, unlike English, formal pronouns signify formal relationships. In English the pronoun "you" is just that, whether you're the president of the United States or my wife.
- The various cultural groups to which you belong have, in a looser sense, their own language or communication traditions. *"Our language is not a written language, which is why oral communication and storytelling*

*are the main vehicles for communicating with others." "My culture communicates as much through silence as through the spoken word." "Mine is a bottom-line language. I say what I mean, and I mean what I say. I wish others could be as clear and direct."*

- Notice what topics your cultures permit and forbid. *"Many members of my family died in the Holocaust. It was only as an adult that I learned this. To this day, none of the survivors will talk about it." "In my family, we wouldn't think of speaking about our age or asking someone about her illness."*

- Most of us use language for different purposes in different settings. Some cultures value brevity and language that gets right to the point. Others prefer layered narratives that take as long as they need to. *"In medical school we were taught to present a patient as concisely as possible, limiting our discussion of the case to pertinent medical information. Rarely did we ask the patient what she thought was going on or what mattered to her. Either we didn't have time for that or it didn't matter or both."*

- People prefer different media, whether written, visual, or verbal forms of communication. *"If I see one more PowerPoint presentation I'll scream! Why don't they just talk directly to us?" "I hate it when the speaker has no handouts or visual aids to accompany her talk. It's hard to follow."*

### Design the Bridge Together

The goal: Make space at the table for diverse cultural perspectives.

Everyone involved in the decision-making process brings a complex package of cultural influences. You can work with others to bridge differences as the decision requires.

#### Plan Ahead

As you build the decision-making table, ask yourself, *"**Who** should be here? **Where** and **when** should we meet? **How** should we talk together?"* As you make your plans, anticipate how others might answer these questions. When you meet, test your assumptions and check with the participants about how they see their roles, whether the time and space allotted are satisfactory, and how the dialogue should run.

*"I am the uncle, and I will be speaking for the family."*

*"Is there anyone else who should be here?"*

*"I hope we are not bound by the clock so we can spend as much time as needed to work things out."*

*"I selected this room, away from the hospital, so we can have an extended, private, and uninterrupted conversation."*

*"Perhaps you, as Johnny's parents, can start us off. What's on your mind?"*

### Share the Right of Way

The goal: Insure broad and full participation in the decision-making process.

Western culture prides itself in cutting to the chase and taking charge. Cultures that emphasize preliminary rituals of establishing context and relationships before plunging into substantive discussion have something to teach.

*"Before we get started, I hope everyone will feel free to speak and share views. My role is to make and to hold the space for this to happen."*

### Take a Manageable Risk

To break through suspicion, make a respectful overture to others. This can take the form of acknowledging one's own cultural bias, perhaps even admitting a previous oversight or mistake.

*"In our medical culture, we often forget to slow down and listen. I realize I haven't asked you directly about what Johnny's deafness means to you and your family."*

*"As a Navajo, a woman, and a medical doctor, I am caught up in several cultures that don't always fit together easily."*

### Build Confidence

Start slowly and refrain from jumping to the decision-making stage to build trust. You get to know others first as people with important values. Before confronting them with opposing options, you begin to see why they approach the issue as they do.

*"For us, being Deaf is not just a medical label. It's who we are."*

### Find Common Ground

Acknowledge differences but look at them through the lens of commonality. You can dissolve tension, not by ignoring or dismissing differences, but by looking at them from the perspective of mutuality. Real and perceived differences can coexist with shared needs, interests, and unique characteristics.

*"Even though you and I come from very different cultures, we're both physicians. Let's see where we agree."*

## A Tale of Two Families. . .Concluded

Caroline understood Baby Marie's extended family. She knew that they visited when they had a ride from their home, over 200 miles away, and that their return home depended on their ride. Their place was with the baby, and they stayed with her while they could. She also knew that, because of language and culture, they understood little of the hospital environment, and the physicians and nurses knew even less about them.

The next time the family visited, Caroline asked the attending physician if she could offer to meet alone with the family. Dr. Walsh said yes.

The family (eight in number) agreed. Caroline spoke to the uncle, in his own language. "Good afternoon. Thank you for coming. It's good to see you all again. I am concerned that we haven't done a good job of answering your questions and making you feel comfortable when you come to visit. I'd like to listen to you, if I may. This afternoon I have as long as you'd like to spend with me. I hope that I can reassure you that we are doing our very best for your baby."

For the next hour, various family members spoke, Caroline mostly listened, and when the questions ended, she said, "I know that hospital time and Anglo time are not Navajo time. I, too, struggle with this. Let me tell you what worries me. As long as Baby Marie stays in the hospital, she will live in our time. Have you thought about taking her home and letting her live according to your time, however long or short that might be?"

The family was quiet, and the uncle asked if they could be alone. Caroline left the room. Thirty minutes later, the uncle asked her back in and spoke for the family.

"We have decided that Marie should live according to God's time. We have a ride back home later this evening. We would like to take her with us. We will wrap her in a warm blanket. Can you help us do that?"

✻ ✻ ✻ ✻ ✻ ✻ ✻ ✻ ✻ ✻ ✻ ✻ ✻ ✻ ✻ ✻ ✻ ✻ ✻ ✻ ✻ ✻ ✻ ✻ ✻ ✻ ✻ ✻ ✻ ✻ ✻ ✻ ✻ ✻ ✻ ✻

Dan White, following the judge's advice, met with the hospital's interpreters and with the staff at the Cochlear Implant Center (CIC). They explained that for some people in the Deaf community, the issue of cochlear implants for children remains controversial and turns on matters of language and cultural identity as much as medicine.

"If the child's parents are themselves Deaf, they may fear losing their child to the hearing world. Nearly all of the implant centers, especially in the beginning, insisted on an auditory-only approach following surgery. Many still do and forbid any visual communication whatsoever. Deaf parents who signed found themselves unable to communicate with their children.

More recently, families and physicians have begun to collaborate on ways to get the most out of the implant by maintaining the child's sign language. There is a risk that, if a child does not develop spoken-language skills after a cochlear implant, prohibiting sign language may leave that child permanently developmentally delayed. While the medical issues are real, so are the language and identity issues. What have Johnny's parents told you about this?"

The next day, Dan conferred with Johnny's parents. "As you know, yesterday I met with the interpreters and some of the CIC staff. I must say, they opened my eyes to a number of issues beyond just the medical. I am beginning to see how different your perspective must be from mine. I apologize for not asking you this before. Can you tell me what you hope for Johnny and what you fear most? I'll do the same. Let's see what we can work out."

Effective communication respects and expects cultural differences. We reach, teach, and learn across cultures—our own and others'—every day. As we learn to move easily among cultures, we negotiate different and often conflicting rituals, codes, rules, and behavioral norms. In the end, we reconcile very different accounts of reality. The ability to navigate a cross-cultural environment is a basic social skill necessary for everyday survival, not just exotic expertise limited to world travelers or foreign diplomats. When the choices are tough and the stakes are high, effective decision-makers attend to important cultural realities.

# 8

## Navigate in Organizations

*The culture of organization runs strongly to the shifting of problems to others—to an escape from mental effort and personal responsibility. This, in turn, becomes the larger public attitude. It is for others to do the worrying, take the action. In the world of the great organization, problems are not solved, but passed on.*

**John Kenneth Galbraith**

From *Dilbert*'s private-sector cubicles to government agencies, veterans of life in organizations know the pain and frustration of the problem that is passed along. Accountable leadership seems to be in short supply. Employees get pink slips, and CEOs get golden parachutes. Shareholders get profits, and communities get waste sites. Instead of, *"The buck stops here,"* we hear a public relations message, *"I have convened a blue-ribbon committee to recommend appropriate action."*

Powerful habits of deciding, acting, and communicating create an ingrained culture that is highly resistant to change. When new employees or volunteers join an organization, they mold their behavior and expectations to this culture, either because of encouragement or because of discipline.

This chapter focuses on decision-making within organizations. We describe **obstacles** on the road to a good decision, such as time constraints and unhealthy cultural norms for discourse; we examine **leaders' habits and behaviors** that promote good decision-making; and we advocate the importance of establishing a **climate of reflection** in even the most fast-paced, crisis-driven work environments. We show how leaders can create and sustain integrity—comprehensiveness, coherence, and transparency—in their decisions.

## MONEY AND MISSION

Odyssey Inc. works with street kids—at-risk youth wrestling with drug addiction, alcoholism, homelessness, suicide, and violence. Three weeks ago, following the last board meeting, executive director Randy Lovett spoke with a reporter for the *McClellan Gazette*: "The news is grim," she told him. "An outside accounting firm has confirmed that, absent a miracle, we're going to have to close our halfway house and cut the rest of our programs by 75 percent in the next sixty days. Cutbacks at the local, state, and federal levels have killed us. I don't know what's going to happen to these kids."

Max Long, a prominent local businessman, read the article and immediately called board chair Don Abeyta. "I'd like to donate $100,000 per year for three years to Odyssey. I've been there. I know what these kids face. Now I'm in a position to help them."

For the first time in months, Don Abeyta was upbeat as he called the board meeting to order. "Mr. Long's donation is unrestricted, so Odyssey can use the funds as it sees fit. His donation is not only generous, but basically it comes with no strings attached. All he asks is that we publicly acknowledge his gift. He'd like to present the first check during a press conference to be held at his office. I assured him we'd be happy to talk to our media contacts and guarantee maximum coverage."

Abeyta's announcement ignited a buzz of excitement among the board members. Mary Lewis, however, was silent. Finally she broke in: "I wonder if you're aware that Max Long owns more than one business. We all know about his truck dealership, but he's also heavily invested in Brody's beer and liquor distributorship—that sells the very products our kids abuse. And I happen to know that last year he acquired ownership of a waste management company that has twice been indicted for toxic waste dumping. Nothing came of those charges, but the State Environment Department is still investigating him for possible contamination of the city's water supply. What if this donation is designed to distract attention away from his legal problems? Even if he isn't using us and our kids, do we really want dirty money?"

What's the right thing to do? Is this a choice between avoiding the appearance of impropriety on the one hand and helping, maybe even saving, young people in trouble on the other? What does integrity call for in this situation? Such tough choices occur daily in the world of nonprofit organizations, businesses, and government agencies.

## BASIC OBSTACLES TO INTEGRITY

### Time as Adversary

In our work with organizations, large and small, private and public, we have discovered one constant. In all of them, the first and most often-cited barrier to thoughtful and careful decision-making is the same: time, or rather, the lack of it.

*"Time is always against us. We must make important decisions as quickly as possible."*

*"We can't pull together all the people we'd like to, because we don't have time."*

*"We don't have time to double-check information and assumptions."*

*"We have to fight our way to a con-*clusion by checking our options and doing the best we can in the time we have."

*"We have other urgent demands waiting in line, so we just can't take more time."*

> *Half the trouble in this world comes from saying "yes" too quick, and "no" not soon enough.*
>
> **American saying**

When we bow to such time pressure, we don't listen carefully to diverse viewpoints; we shortchange or even omit a thoughtful discussion of what is truly important, and we don't prepare and deliver an honest account to those affected. We just decide and move on to the next urgent matter.

Effective decision-makers are not seduced by the first attractive option that comes along. They resist the pressure of time in two ways. First, they test the assumption that time is limited. Sometimes that assumption is false. Sometimes it is partially true, but there is more time than originally thought—time to slow down. Sometimes they craft a provisional or interim decision that removes the urgency and buys time to make a more considered, permanent decision.

Second, when the time to decide is truly limited, they compress the five decision steps (from Chapters 1 to 5) to leverage the time available. For example, they go directly to a discussion of values.

Randy Lovett could feel the tension escalating between Abeyta and Lewis. She said, "Okay, let's slow things down here. Mary, we'll want to hear more about your concerns—and for that matter, what each of you thinks is of central importance regarding this issue. But before this conversation runs away with us, let's acknowledge that this is a major fork in the road for our organization. We need to think through all its aspects. How much time do we have before we must give Mr. Long our response?"

Randy's instinct is a good one. The Odyssey board and staff need to talk about how to talk. Her question about pace tests the urgency to solve the looming financial crisis. Is it as real as people feel? When we slow down, even a little, we may be able to see what is missing, such as additional information or people who deserve to be included, or at least considered.

When we frame time as our adversary, we naturally feel pushed to respond instinctively. If we need to make a snap, intuitive judgment, this approach usually serves us well. But when important, complicated choices present themselves, we can adjust our relationship to time. Reflection rather than reaction leads to better decisions.

> *At times it is folly to hasten, at other times to delay. The wise do everything in its proper time.*
>
> **Ovid**

When the situation calls for an immediate decision, we can incorporate reflection, even under pressure. Certain professionals such as emergency medical personnel, military leaders, police, and fire chiefs often have to make crucial, even life-and-death decisions on the spot. For them, past experience forms the curriculum that teaches them how to respond. They have internalized lessons learned from challenging situations and are trained to recognize and respond to similar crises instantly, without having to start from scratch. Careful deliberation from the past can enter and enhance a current decision, when there is no time for reflection. Time need not be the enemy.

### Patterns of Behavior

As with individuals, every organization has a culture that shapes, and often controls, how people share information and make decisions. This culture may be complex or simple, with its roots clear or shrouded in legend and the mists of time. Like Odyssey, many mission-driven nonprofits are cut from the same cloth as their founder, perhaps a charismatic leader who shaped the organization's growth and attracted staff who shared the same vision and business philosophy. By contrast, large organizations such as government agencies and major corporations are shaped more by the times and the nature of the work performed than by any one leader.

A large organization whose decision-making habits continue to make news is the National Aeronautics and Space Administration (NASA). Following the catastrophic loss of the space shuttles Challenger and Columbia, government oversight committees, congressional hearings, and media investigators have examined NASA's decision-making. These inquiries revealed a flawed decision-making culture that discouraged honest reflection and a healthy exchange of information.

- Because of NASA's strong hierarchical organization, people deferred to authority in ways that limited the open and honest expression of different opinions.

- The group that evaluated the shuttle Columbia and assessed the risk of its missing heat tiles did not encourage all those involved to speak freely. Nor did it seek out, collect, or analyze different opinions.

- The senior person present during any discussion tightly controlled the flow of conversation, as is typical of hierarchical organizations.

NASA's culture of controlled discussion sent a message: *"We don't really want to know what you think. Be careful in offering strong opinions out of step with the way we do things here."* NASA's norms and decision-making habits cut off access to the information and robust dialogue that might have prevented catastrophe.

When people in an organization face a tough choice, the culture's stamp can be especially powerful. In an atmosphere of pressure and crisis, cultural norms function like the autopilot on an airplane, kicking in to carry decision-makers to a conclusion at the expense of deeper, authentic conversation.

Ingrained cultural norms form an organization's identity and take integrity and virtue as givens. *"We are committed to this organization. We are good people. Whatever we do, we do with integrity."* This mindset almost guarantees that blind spots, gaps in our awareness, will persist.

> *People just starting their careers may think a job is just a job. But when they choose a company, they often choose a way of life.*
> **Terrence Deal and Allan Kennedy**

Consider a large organization devoted to scientific and engineering research, one that prizes rigorous analysis. So long as the topics are technical and business related, bruising debate about facts is not only permitted, it's expected. Yet, stray outside this bandwidth of comfort and you feel the tension in the room. Posters extolling core values such as respect for employees and leadership integrity may adorn the walls, but the vocabulary and skills to bring these values to bear on important business, scientific, and engineering decisions are conspicuously absent.

> *In general, the more sophisticated the organization, the greater is its efficiency—but also its vulnerability.*
> **Edward Luttwak**

Integrity has less to do with good intentions and more to do with the depth and scope of the decision-making process. Organizational culture and untested assumptions about virtue and integrity make it possible for good people to make bad decisions.

Returning to our case, let's look deeper into Odyssey's culture. What habits, what styles of leadership influence conversation around a tough choice?

Ten years ago Mahlon Williams founded Odyssey Inc. to offer a lifeline to impoverished street youth. Williams was himself a product of the streets. His charisma, energy, and risk-taking had earned him leadership of a gang at sixteen and a stretch in prison for armed robbery by twenty. Upon his release, Williams channeled those same qualities into building a company dedicated to providing shelter, aid, and above all, hope, to disadvantaged youth—people like himself who sought escape from spiraling cycles of poverty, violence, and addiction. In the beginning, he **was** the organization. He handpicked his staff and every member of the original board, and they were proud to follow his lead. His fund-raising appeals were electric, community money poured in, and outreach programs, education facilities, and a halfway house became realities. Over the years, hundreds of kids passed through Odyssey's programs and embarked on paths to brighter futures. Buoyed by success, Williams began to dream bigger. If hundreds of kids could be saved, why not thousands? Why not tens of thousands? Later, he would admit that the business side of the enterprise bored him, especially as it grew more complex. Records were poorly kept or lost, funds were mismanaged, and suddenly Williams found himself overexpanded, overextended, and well over budget.

Now, as we have seen, Odyssey teeters on the brink of financial disaster. Three months ago, in sorrow and disappointment, Williams resigned. Randy Lovett has been on the job for two months. In all the important ways, however, the culture and habits of Odyssey are still those of its founder.

Odyssey now needs a different kind of leader, one who can engage others in a new conversation. Charisma and "seat of the pants" are not enough. The dialogue must deepen. Odyssey's eight board members and the new executive director need to find a way to talk about what matters. Let's listen in on their discussion.

Don Abeyta: "Mary, what's the point of going on if we can't serve these kids? I am aware of Long's somewhat shady reputation. But the money he's donating is legally acquired, and our use of it is honorable. You'd have to be crazy to look **this** gift horse in the mouth."

Mary Lewis: "I resent it when you take that snide tone with me. I am neither crazy nor stupid. Ever since Mahlon resigned, you've been acting as if you founded this organization and the rest of us are supposed to line up behind you, the way everyone did with Mahlon. Times have changed, and this board needs to change with them! Our job here is not to guess what Mahlon might have done. It's to proceed as efficiently and ethically as possible."

Sometimes a crisis reveals buried conflict running like a fault line through a relationship, invisible, waiting to crack. Unspoken issues about board leadership, ways of treating each other, and established patterns of discussion all surface in this short exchange.

> If someone tells you he is going to make a "realistic decision," you immediately understand that he has resolved to do something bad.
> **Mary McCarthy**

Each organization has a particular set of habits and behavioral norms. However, some patterns are common to all types of organizations. One of the patterns that affects decision-making is groupthink, a phenomenon that leads inevitably to the deterioration of a group's mental efficiency, attention, and judgment. The psychological foundation of groupthink lies in the desire to reduce anxiety and preserve self-esteem. To satisfy these desires, group members encourage a sense of unanimity and discourage dissent. *"We're all in this together."* Through a series of unspoken agreements, we move the discussion toward a comfortable, though flawed, decision.

Look for patterns that may be signs your group is heading toward the groupthink trap.

---

### Groupthink Signs

- **Illusion of invulnerability**
  *"Nothing can hurt us as a result of this decision."*

- **Illusion of unanimity**
  *"We all support this decision, don't we?"*

- **Rationalization**
  *"Now that we know what we're doing, how shall we explain this to others?"*

- **Ethical blinders**
  *"We'd never do anything to hurt the environment. We live here, too."*

- **Stereotyping others outside the group**
  *"They're just a bunch of naysayers with an agenda. Why should we listen to them?"*

- **Dismissal of facts that challenge preferred choice**
  *"Don't overthink this. We know what we need to do to move forward."*

- **Failure to:**
  - consider values implicit in the alternatives
  - talk about the full range of alternatives
  - consider drawbacks of choices
  - consult knowledgeable outsiders.

---

## LEADERS AND GOOD DECISIONS

### Habits That Hinder

People usually do not end up in positions of leadership by accident. Some combination of desire and circumstance moves them into that role and shapes their approach to decision-making. While leaders come in all shapes, sizes, colors, and personality types, we have noticed three tendencies that hinder their willingness to invite reflection on values.

**Leaders are more comfortable in charge.** Experienced leaders know how they like to lead and make decisions. Some feel that maintaining tight control is the only way to insure a good outcome. They fear that expanding the decision-making process invites unnecessary complication and chaos. They tend to hold high-stakes decisions close to the vest, letting others in only

> *Isolation is the worst possible counselor.*
> **Miguel de Unamuno**

when they've made their decision. *"I don't have time to deal with the contention and controversy that come when too many people are involved."*

**Leaders like to solve problems.** Some of us are born problem solvers. We've succeeded as leaders, at least partly because we know how to address and work through issues. Remember presidential candidate Ross Perot's answer to the question, *"How would you fix Social Security?" "Social Security. Social Security. Let's just get under the hood and fix it."* Natural problems solvers move immediately to options and begin to shape a solution.

**Leaders are confident and decisive.** Leaders self-select for confidence. They often resist consultation with others for several reasons: a belief that their judgment is better than others, a sense of entitlement that leads them to protect their position of authority, or a fear that involving others signals weakness or indecisiveness. A companion to

> *Nothing discloses real character like the use of power.*
> **Robert G. Ingersoll**

such confidence is the desire to persuade others of the merits of a decision. As we discussed in Chapter 5, this sales or spin approach to communicating with others may sell the decision in the short term, but at tremendous cost to personal credibility in the long term.

A leader's behavior sets the tone for the organization. Personal style and behavior send a powerful message throughout the organization about what is desirable, approved, and safe. Fear of opposition from subordinates, a natural inclination to avoid conflict, and understandable risk-avoidance behavior are all habits that get in the way of creating a culture of openness and accountability. Transparency throughout the decision-making process can be risky. It opens a window onto motive and intent. However, good decisions thrive on fresh air.

Her predecessor at Odyssey created a culture of impatience and action. In contrast, before Randy Lovett joined Odyssey, she was a leader in an organization that valued consultation and collaboration. Now, in the midst of crisis, Odyssey needs a real conversation. There is no solo charismatic leader to line up behind. Inserting herself into the confrontation between Don and Mary, she shows her style. "Look, you're both making good points, and we all need to listen and evaluate them.

The problem is that the nature of the discussion makes it difficult to hear what is really important to you. So let's all take a deep breath, slow down, and move ahead attentively and respectfully. If we do that, I'm confident we'll make a good decision."

> *The laurel will go to the leader who encourages healthy dissent and values those followers brave enough to say no. The successful leader will have, not the loudest voice, but the readiest ear.*
> **Warren Bennis**

### Habits That Help

Randy Lovett's behavior and example may begin an important shift in the way Odyssey addresses tough choices. Over time, her habits may affect the way others behave.

There are several ways a leader can signal that she and the organization are serious about openness, transparency, and accountability. First, she must be willing to hear hard things and accept that diverse, sometimes discordant opinions will surface. She must be able to live with discomfort, knowing that openness and the anxiety it produces are worth the cost.

"Mary, I think most of us would love to take this donation, which would allow us to carry on without cutting vital programs and turning away needy kids. I know you care as deeply as we do about our mission. Help us all see this through your eyes. What is it about Max Long's business and his reputation that may hurt us if we take the money?"

When leaders respond to dissonant, even strident voices with respect and open a dialogue, everyone who witnesses or hears about the encounter receives the message, *"It's okay to speak up."* In our experience, this kind of response demonstrates strength and purpose. It does not cave into or attempt to appease aggressive behavior. Respect and dialogue can still end in disagreement, but what a difference a bit of dialogue makes.

Don: "Mary, if the consequences for the kids we serve were any less dire, I might agree with you. Max Long may be using us in some way, and I take your point about his unsavory environmental record. But tobacco company money is being used for smoking cessation problems. Why can't Max Long's liquor company profits be used to help kids with alcohol problems? I don't see why we can't accept the money **and** do some good with it."

> *Divorced from ethics, leadership is reduced to management and politics to mere technique.*
> **James MacGregor Burns**

Another signal leaders can send is an authentic commitment to values and a genuine concern for stakeholders. This requires more than an organization mission statement filled with rhetoric about the importance of employees, customers, or the community. Too seldom does this rhetoric make an appearance at the decision-making table.

Are leaders prepared to live the organization's core values and their own important personal values, even when it is inconvenient or costly to do so? Maintaining trust and credibility often require this. This is when a leader and an organization are tested. Listen in as the Odyssey board considers stakeholders.

> Another board member, Val McIntire, weighs in. "Mahlon built this agency from nothing with grit, passion, and a silver tongue. But there are really dedicated staff, too. They know the families and the kids in ways we never will. Before we decide anything, I'd like to bring them in on this decision. Randy, can we convene a meeting with senior staff before the end of the week to recap the story and get their feedback before we accept or turn down the donation?"

> *A genuine leader is not a searcher for consensus, but a molder of consensus.*
> **Martin Luther King Jr.**

Leaders can follow through on what they have heard from and about stakeholders. Do they regularly let others know they have been heard and understood? This is not about agreement but a fair hearing. Are they comfortable being open and possibly influenced or even changed by what they hear?

Leaders can insure that systems and practices are in place to communicate important decisions back to staff and others who are affected. Accountability requires that leaders own their decisions and that others understand why the decisions were made. Leaders demonstrate authenticity and honesty when they acknowledge their struggle, avoid unwarranted claims of certainty, and admit doubt. From authenticity and honesty comes credibility.

See the "Organizational Values Survey" in the Appendix as a tool for discovering what employees value and how they assess their leaders' credibility.

---

### What Leaders Can Do

- Take advantage of defining moments.
- Admit that you struggle and have doubts.
- Encourage others to use values to make decisions.
- Accept outspokenness without punishment or retaliation.
- Acknowledge feedback received by letting others know what was done with it.
- Promote a common language for discussing values.
- Be an ambassador for the organization's mission and values.

## ESTABLISHING A CLIMATE OF REFLECTION

### *Overall Strategies*

If leaders reach beyond their ingrained habits, there are a number of strategies at their disposal to increase decision-making quality. What these strategies have in common is creating reflective space: whether it's before or after your decision becomes public, the more you listen, consider others, and open up, the more likely it is that others will accept and support your decision.

Let's start toward the end of the decision process. Without exception, the single biggest decision-making failure we encounter in organizations is not the decision itself but the failure to communicate effectively. The reasons? Fear of a hostile response, time as an adversary, and uncertainty about the best way to communicate. The result? A good decision may go off track.

As soon as others hear about the decision, stories spread like wildfire. Support either coalesces or dissolves. Opposition surfaces. Perhaps the most effective way to improve the overall climate of decision-making is to communicate well. Who needs to be the first to hear about the decision? What do they need to know? Timely communication back to staff is critical. Whenever possible, report important decisions directly and honestly to those affected. Let time constraints and other situational factors suggest the appropriate method, but not at the expense of good communication. You may distribute a memo, speak at a staff meeting, or send an e-mail. However you choose to communicate, make certain the message is adequately comprehensive and always genuine.

Another strategy is to incorporate some version of the steps outlined in Chapters 1 through 5 into daily dialogue and activity. Whether yours is a large corporation or a local church, make it your habit to ask, "*What is important to you about this issue?*" Anyone can ask the question. If you do so in a meeting, already you will have taken the discussion to a deeper reflective level than usually occurs in our time-diseased culture.

> Three days later at Odyssey's administrative offices. . .
> Randy Lovett: "Thank you for coming. This is a first for our board, to consult directly with staff. In the past, all the communication between board members and staff filtered through Mahlon. I invited the six of you because you are our most senior and experienced managers. Four of you have been with Odyssey from the very beginning. You understand our mission and our clients better than anyone else does. You know Don, Mary, and Val, all members of our board. At the last board meeting, we agreed to consult with key staff to get your views about an important decision facing us all."

Another strategy is for leaders themselves to raise the core value question. It is up to leaders to show the way and educate others. A CEO sends a strong message when she asks the senior management team to pull out the corporate mission statement and use it in the discussion. When a board of directors, reviewing next year's budget, asks the executive director what values she used to allocate scarce resources, they both now have important language to use when they explain the budget to the staff. It is hard for staff and employees to do this on their own. It may be seen as subversive. This concern keeps people silent, but a leader can show the way.

Leaders tend to look for dramatic and bold action steps. In fact, there is surprising power in small, meaningful acts. Effective leaders find modest, ordinary ways to intentionally address values by creating reflective space. Over the years, our clients have reported to us that leaders who initiate real change operate within their sphere of influence and remain under the radar. Change happens because leaders begin to ask key questions about values. They announce their decisions differently, request that those who report to them explain their values, and always reflect back what they hear. These daily practices are the strategies that make a difference.

There are also high-profile decisions, like the one Odyssey faces. The risks are great, and so are the opportunities, especially the opportunity to send an unforgettable message to all who are watching to see how the organization uses values and makes tough choices.

Consider a community-based organization serving the health care needs of the homeless. The loyal staff works long hours for modest pay. They understand that this year the budget provides a modest amount of money for staff raises. A common criticism of today's corporate leadership is the size of executive pay. *"They always look out for number one. All this talk about concern for employees is so much . . . rhetoric. It's certainly not reality."* What if the agency leaders decided to forgo their own raises and use that money to increase the wages of the lowest-paid people in the organization? That would send an unforgettable message.

Today, the climate of decision-making is difficult. People feel stretched to the limit. Whether it's a lean, downsized corporation or an understaffed, underfunded nonprofit organization addressing overwhelming social needs, the time pressure they experience is real. Creating reflective space seems like a luxury. If, in an effort to improve decision-making, leaders launch a new initiative, they should consider the following criteria:

- The method is simple and easy to use.
- The method makes sense to time-pressured, outcome-oriented leaders and managers because it:
  - emphasizes action more than concept
  - offers results
  - uses time efficiently
  - can be scaled up or down to fit the time constraints and circumstances of different situations.

- People need opportunities to practice new behaviors, using real problems.
- There is ongoing support for people who feel tentative or awkward with the method, to help them learn to use it with confidence.

Finally, a word about compliance. Leaders and governing boards need to do a better job of keeping the language of ethics separate from the language of compliance. If we want our government institutions, corporations, and nonprofit organizations to thrive and strive for integrity in all decisions,

> *Ethical truth is as exact and peremptory as physical truth.*
> **Herbert Spencer**

the sense of what is ethical and good must not be "dumbed down" to compliance.

Satisfying the minimum requirements of law or regulation does not inspire or encourage people to do their best. But there is a more insidious impact. When the orientation is upon compliance, this can send a message that it is acceptable to walk the line of illegality or rule-breaking as long as you stay "just inside the line." The collapse of Enron, run by the so-called "smartest guys in the room," is a cautionary tale of an organizational culture that took pride in its ability to play with the edges of what was legally permissible.

It is likely, if not inevitable, that there will continue to be ethics offices, compliance directors, and ethics audits. These worthy activities are necessary but not sufficient to guarantee that an organization is really committed to integrity in decision-making. A corporation may state in its mission and core values that it cares for its employees and serves the communities where it operates. But if leaders make a strategic decision to lobby for weakening laws and regulations governing air quality and worker safety, the disconnect between advertised values and reality is substantial. The bar of integrity is usually quite a bit higher than the bar of compliance.

## Small Group Behavior

In every organization, small groups make decisions. Boards, management teams, project members, and committees meet to address issues, offer recommendations, solve problems, and make decisions. If an initiative to increase openness and integrity fails at the local, group level, it will fail throughout the organization, no matter how charismatic or enthusiastic the leader might be.

In a remarkable book titled *The Wisdom of Crowds,* James Surowiecki examines what makes groups smart and dumb. He discusses the conditions necessary for a group to harness multiple perspectives and make a decision that is better than any individual could make alone. He concludes that there

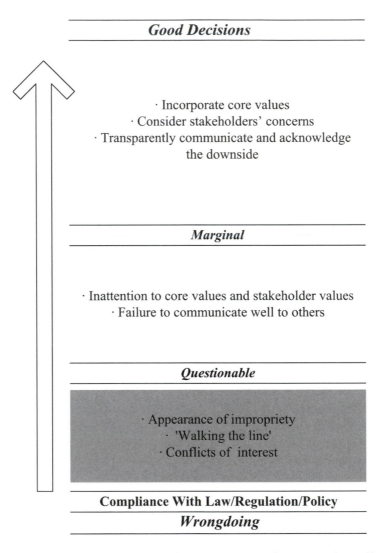

**"Raising the Bar"- Beyond Compliance**

*Good Decisions*

· Incorporate core values
· Consider stakeholders' concerns
· Transparently communicate and acknowledge
the downside

*Marginal*

· Inattention to core values and stakeholder values
· Failure to communicate well to others

*Questionable*

· Appearance of impropriety
· 'Walking the line'
· Conflicts of interest

**Compliance With Law/Regulation/Policy**

*Wrongdoing*

are a number of key variables in the way a group functions that affect its capacity to be smart:

- The group needs to be cognitively diverse, so different perspectives can shape the decision.
- People need to think and act as independently as possible, so their unique perspectives are not unduly influenced by the views of others and remain available to all.

- The group members need to operate without direction or dictation of the answer by higher authority so their genuine views form the basis of the decision.

- The group needs a workable structure to elicit the differing views, summarize them, and shape them into an outcome.

When these conditions are met, everyone in the group works harder, thinks smarter, and reaches better conclusions. Surowiecki's book describes the what but not the how.

Leaders and managers in organizations can assist and encourage their small decision-making groups to get the best out of everyone. To do so, they must recognize and change group dynamics that discourage dialogue. Consider the structural characteristics and behaviors in the following table:

> *There is one person who is smarter than anybody and that is everybody.*
> Talleyrand

---

### Group Dynamics Affecting Dialogue

- **Size of group**
  If it's too large, some are uncomfortable speaking; if too small, there is no cognitive diversity.

- **Speaking order**
  When those with power speak early and strongly, others may defer and withhold important, diverse views.

- **Debate mode**
  When listening is poor, acknowledgement lacking, and criticism or putdowns of ideas common, people stay silent rather than get "beat up."

- **Too prescriptive**
  When the line is crossed from passion (what I strongly believe) to prescription (what absolutely must happen), people shut down.

- **Punishment**
  When those in authority express disapproval verbally or nonverbally, cut others off, fail to invite the outspoken ones to the next meeting, or schedule a meeting when they can't attend, they foster a climate of fear.

- **Conspiracy of comfort**
  Verbal and nonverbal messages remind everyone about what is expected, and uncomfortable truths remain unspoken.

- **Dominance**
  Individuals take over the discussion, posture with strong statements, or pressure others to submit.

With so much arrayed against openness and honest exchange, we need clear microstrategies to improve group functioning at all levels. The four approaches that follow, provide the "how."

> *It is better to light one candle than to curse the darkness.*
> **Chinese proverb**

## WHAT YOU CAN DO

The goal: Develop an organizational culture with habits and behaviors that encourage openness, reflection, and integrity in decision-making.

### Build Safety in the Group Container

Make it clear that everyone is valued and everyone's opinions will be heard and considered. Take responsibility for enforcing the simple ground rule of respect. Passionate disagreement and vigorous discussion can remain respectful.

Randy: "Before we get into the issue, I'll explain that we have set aside an hour for our discussion with you. The board members and I want to hear from each of you directly, so I'll need your help in making that happen. You may hear others express something you disagree with. I am less interested in whether you disagree than with what you think is important, so please keep the focus on your own ideas and concerns. Let's start by going around the table and letting everyone state their initial thoughts. After each staffer has had a say, we'll open it up for discussion."

Ask yourself the following questions to check the safety level in the decision space:

- Is the order of speaking or the amount of speaking reducing the overall level of participation you need?
- Do you need more structure, such as the help of a facilitator, or some ground rules to engage multiple views, get difficult truths on the table, and identify important values?
- Can people come together without overreaction and polarization?
- Does the interaction leave people feeling heard and respected by others?

### Nurture Clarity and Depth in the Conversation

During the time available, ask people to go beyond values jargon and explain what these words mean in this situation. Treat impassioned statements as opportunities to learn what lies behind the emotion or the strong position.

Jane Williams, longtime, dedicated staffer: "Randy, I don't know why we are even having this discussion. It's a no-brainer! We are in the 'saving kids' business, not the 'splitting ethical hairs' business! It makes me question why you all are on the board if that isn't clear to you."

Randy: "Jane, just to be clear—it sounds as though you feel so strongly about accepting the money because of your absolute commitment to helping, in some cases saving, young people's lives."

Ask the following questions to check the quality of the conversation with participants:

- Am I getting clearer about what is involved here?
- Have I heard from everyone about what is important?
- What are we missing that hasn't been addressed?
- What do we need to understand better, that others could speak to?

### Attend to Accountability for the Decision

Be completely clear who is making the decision and who will stand in support of it. Decision-makers must know the real values that guided their decision so they can be prepared to communicate these truthfully to others. When decision-makers carefully identify and weigh the decision's effects, before they commit to a final course of action, they can honestly state that they did their best.

#### At the end of the meeting. . .

Don Abeyta: "Thank you all for your directness and your clarity about what is important to you. I want to remind you that this is not any one person's decision, but a decision that the board will make. We like to act with unanimity when possible, but this issue may require that we vote. I will make two commitments to you tonight. First, Mary, Val, and I will relay your concerns to the whole board. Second, no matter how the board comes down on this issue, we will address all of your concerns and the role they played in our decision."

Ask yourself the following questions to assess the fullness of the decision:

- Are you clear who owns the decision and who will stand with the owners in support?
- Does the quality of the decision process permit those who disagree with the outcome to support the integrity of the decision, despite their differences?
- Are you prepared to articulate the common ground of values that support the integrity of the decision?

- Are you willing to be accountable to stakeholders by being transparent and clear about how your decision will affect them?

**One week later at the Odyssey board meeting...**

Don Abeyta: "I know we have taken a formal vote, but I want to sum up my sense of our discussion. The bottom line is that the board has voted to accept Max Long's offer. We do so because we believe that continuing to serve as many at-risk youth as possible is the heart and soul of our mission. As the unanimous sentiment of the senior staff made clear, nothing should be more important to us than that. We accept this money with our eyes open, recognizing that the donor's motivation may be as much to enhance his own reputation as to help us. The current controversy surrounding the donor and his businesses could very well raise questions about our organizational integrity in the minds of our supporters. We cannot control this. But we can anticipate community reaction and explain our mission and decision clearly and honestly."

## Transfer Learning

Learn from the process, and use it in other situations. Culture shifts and new norms take root with repeated practice. In this way, your experience can inform the next opportunity.

**Three weeks after the board decision...**

Don Abeyta: "Randy, on behalf of the entire board, I want to thank you for encouraging us to have a deeper conversation with the staff and with each other."

Randy: "Thank you, Don. It worked out well for all of us, and I think we emerged with a better sense of who we all are and what we're about. Now that we have some budget breathing room, I have some ideas about continuing board-staff exchanges. Every April, the board holds a strategic planning retreat, and I would love to kick it off with a board-staff round table, where staff can float their ideas and stimulate board thinking about agency direction. If we hired a good group facilitator, I think a three-hour session could generate a lot of useful input."

## ADDITIONAL TOOLS

In the Appendix there is a decision tree, "When to Use a Values Process," to help leaders identify situations that call for an intentional process to initiate values-based decision-making. See also "Using the Steps in Your Organization" for an overview of the process at work. See also the "How to Use the 'On-the-Fly'" worksheet for tips on how to compress the process when time is limited. In a larger, more complex organization that wants to grow a culture of integrity, the "Organizational Values Survey" and the "Map Stakeholder Values" worksheets offer a way to discover how key stakeholders view managerial and leadership decision-making.

# 9

## Reach Your Destination: Lean into the Light

*If there is a stage at which an individual life becomes truly adult, it must be when one grasps the irony in its unfolding and accepts responsibility for a life lived in the midst of such paradox. . . . There are simply no answers to some of the great pressing questions. You continue to live them out, making your life a worthy expression of leaning into the light.*

**Barry Lopez**

Like it or not, life is about choices. We have invoked images of courtyards and buildings, oil slicks, and guiding stars to illustrate the major roles that perspective, dialogue, and values play on the road to a good decision. These images not only stimulate the mind, they also guide us to ground that is solid and practical.

Our field guide explores five steps to good decisions. The ground is firm, though some will see quicksand. *"You're suggesting we throw away our moral compass. It's important to stay the course and be guided by what we know to be true."* We agree that finding and following a guiding star is important. It's just that the work is ongoing. Expanding and shifting one's perspective does not lead to moral relativism. Just the opposite is true. Clear perspective and thorough assessment of values deepen your roots and ground your commitments.

The steps take time. *"We don't have time, and too many voices can lead us astray. Decisions must be clear and timely."* Time constraints are real, and decisions need to be appropriately responsive. Nevertheless, decision-makers who rush their decisions and fail to consult others often make poor decisions that cost even more in time, energy, and money.

When we turn our attention away from right vs. wrong and toward right vs. right, some may see a naiveté about the real world, if not outright moral timidity. *"There are false values and bad people in the world. Moral courage requires that we stand firm, and apart from evil."* That's true. But taking a stand against what is wrong is just the beginning. The more difficult work begins when we move toward what is good. As we look closer and listen better, the territory of important values expands, and we face tough choices between competing goods.

We've tackled the role of values in discourse and decision-making at a time when pundits and politicians hurl moral principles at each other and at us in an endgame of good vs. bad. We live in times of stark choices and dangerous consequences. *"Are you suggesting that we try to see the world through Osama bin Laden's eyes, that we invite him to the negotiation table?"* No. But not everyone with whom we have serious, principled disagreement is Osama bin Laden, or even an enemy or adversary.

When we automatically label people with different perspectives and values as moral inferiors, if not enemies, we foreclose any possibility that we might learn something from them. When we focus only on confronting evil and wrongdoing, we neglect the complexity and vigor of legitimate, competing goods. The road to a good decision is paved with perspectives and values that run deep and wide. For us, this is the terrain of productive though challenging moral discourse.

Values and people clash, but that doesn't mean that one value or person must be right and the other wrong. People and interests can conflict and still be good. Nevertheless, tough choices require that something lead the way in the final decision. When we choose one value over another, a good not chosen does not thereby become a wrong. It's still good. Further, a shift in the leading value, over time and in different circumstances, does not signal rootless relativism. The fact that last month I chose security while today I'm choosing privacy and freedom does not mean that my moral compass is broken. The circumstances may be different, as may I.

A CEO of a community service organization knows that to serve his clients, he has to stay in business, even if this requires letting valued employees go. Whatever decision he makes will bring regret. While he would like to serve clients and support all the staff, it is not possible to do both in this situation.

Most people believe that killing others is wrong. Many also believe that one must protect oneself, one's family, and one's country from harm, death, or destruction, even if it involves killing another. Again, they have to choose, depending on the circumstances.

To frame these principled conflicts only as a struggle between good and evil, right and wrong, trivializes their moral depth. The difficult moral

## The Road to a Good Decision

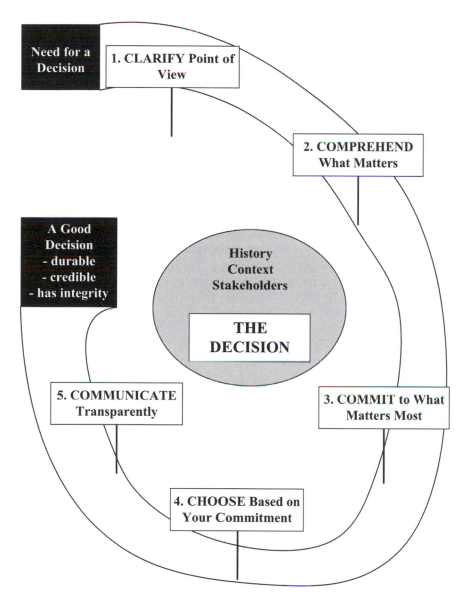

struggle lies in choosing between mutually exclusive, fundamental values. Do I tell the truth or save a life? Do I report domestic violence or respect my client—the victim's request for confidentiality? When I choose one value over another, I may be tempted to dismiss or even turn against the principles

I left behind. I would like to absolve myself from the harm I've done to values that matter.

When we listen carefully to the legitimate demands of competing goods and begin to advocate for one value over another, we're not claiming that the other value suddenly becomes wrong. Important values, especially when they conflict, call on us to commit and choose. Commitment and choice are rarely innocent. They are not harm free. To uphold one good, it may be necessary to lean away from others.

Such conflicts start at home. Before we declare our disagreements with others, we do well to note our internal conflicts. *"I struggle to reconcile my faith, my own experience, and the needs of the broader community. It's not an easy fit."* Throughout this book, we recommend a healthy dose of reflection and self-examination before judging others. Most, if not all, important decisions require that we expose and understand our own values—where they fit well with each other and where they don't. The road to a good decision covers this difficult terrain of competing personal values.

When others join the conversation, we expand the list of values. Our personal list, what matters to us, may or may not grow because of what we hear from others. Regardless, as we move toward a decision, we will choose some values and leave others behind. The temptation to minimize values not chosen, or demonize those who hold them, is powerful. It's also too easy. Moral courage resides in taking responsibility for our regrets. It is hard to hold on to what remains important to us and others, even as we turn toward something else.

What we choose, our guiding values, may change in different situations. Does this mean that no value is permanent? *"Aren't you saying 'anything goes' as you float with the prevailing values of the moment? Don't you understand that right is right and wrong is wrong?"* There are moral options beyond relativism and absolutism. We can do better than laissez-faire ethics, but important truths survive and thrive only inside history, society, and personal realities.

Issues are what they are. The courtyard and the surrounding multistory building don't move. Of course, when I look at an issue, I see it just as I am, from my established position and angle. If I want to see the courtyard from a different perspective, I need others, those beside me and those on the opposite side of the courtyard, to help me see what I can't.

I may visit the courtyard in the morning or evening. This may be my first visit or one of many. The light is always changing. Sometimes there is a crowd; sometimes I'm alone. I may be the same person, but the context is always fresh.

Whether it is core values hanging on the organization's walls, the Ten Commandments, or our profession's code of conduct, values exist in tension, come alive, and assert their meaning only in the present. When they do so and when we pay attention, their force is undeniable.

To the outside observer it may seem that we change our fundamental values from situation to situation. We may change their order of priority from the last time we used them. They may lead us to new and different decisions. We do not, however, extinguish their light.

We have described how decision-makers can travel the road to good decisions. Each of our paths is unique—we cannot navigate by another's landmarks or follow the specific map of their journeys. However, we can make decisions with integrity by following our guiding stars. We can commit to clarity as we consider what matters, coherence when we choose, and candor as we tell others. In these times of mistrust, cynicism, and fear, we can move into the sunshine and fresh air.

We can lean into the light.

# Appendix

## WORKSHEETS AND EXERCISES

## Summary of the Steps

| Step | Activities | Question | Desired Outcome |
|---|---|---|---|
| 1. **Clarify** Perspective | • Stepping Back<br>• Framing | *What point of view do I bring to this decision?* | Improved ability to see clearly and listen effectively |
| 2. **Comprehend** What Matters | • Naming<br>• Dialogue | *What is important to me and others?* | Better understanding of the range of values |
| 3. **Commit** to What Matters Most | • Advocacy<br>• Weighing | *What is most important that should guide our decision?* | A set of guiding values to point the way |
| 4. **Choose** to Act | • Looking at the downside<br>• Considering options | *What is the best fit between importance and action?* | Strong connection between the guiding values and the decision |
| 5. **Communicate** Transparently | • Transparency<br>• Telling the story | *How can I credibly communicate this to others?* | A report of the decision that levels with others about its basis and the consequences |

## Worksheet for Step 1: Clarify Perspective

| | |
|---|---|
| **Introduction** | Framing requires a step back, a look around, and the adjustment of point of view. While this can be accomplished alone, it is helpful to hear how others see differently. When a decision-maker appreciates the range of differing viewpoints early in the process, she: |

- increases the likelihood of meaningful dialogue because participants understand where others are coming from;
- begins to identify biases, prejudgments, and assumptions; and
- notices missing perspectives.

| | |
|---|---|
| **Activity** | When appropriate, consult directly to find out what matters to others. When this is not possible, make an educated guess as to what they would say if asked. |

**Steps to Take**

✎ By yourself, answer the following question: *What is my initial "take" on this decision?* (A take might be an impression, a solution, an assumption, a sense of the kind of the issue this is, or a strong reaction of some kind, e.g., a clear opinion that there is only one thing to do.)

✎ By yourself, also consider whether you bring a particular perspective or point of view to this issue. How would you briefly describe it? It may be a role you play, expertise you possess, or a related experience you have had.

✎ As a group, go around the table and share your frames one at a time. Be brief. Take no more than one to two minutes per person. Listen carefully as others express how they see the situation. Avoid commentary or dialogue *but* follow up with the speaker to clarify anything you do not understand. As you listen, note the different perspectives revealed by these initial takes.

If you have time or the issue is important enough that you must make the time, consider:

**Assumptions:** What are we taking for granted (assumptions) about this decision? Which of these assumptions should we check out to confirm our understanding?
**Other Perspectives:** Do we have necessary perspectives represented here to make a good decision? If not, whom should we involve and how should we involve them?
**Ways to Frame the Decision:** How can we most clearly state the decision we are responsible for making? What does our frame highlight and leave out?
**How to Proceed:** How should we approach the decision (information gathering, consultation, option development, deadline)?

## Asking the Right Questions

| Introduction | Dialogue thrives on questions that encourage openness and depth. The following list is suggestive, not exhaustive. Questions are the creative acts of intelligence. If formulated well, they can open doors, generate valuable information, and lay a firm foundation for thoughtful decision-making. Any one of the following questions may help you understand the values context for your decisions. |
|---|---|

| Uncovering Values | Outcomes |
|---|---|
| *Why is this important to you?* | *What would you like to see come out of this? Why?* |
| *What is important here that we need to look at?* | *What do you hope for?* |
| *What do you think lies at the heart of the matter?* | *What is most meaningful to you in the comments and ideas we have heard up to now?* |
| *What matters to you most in this situation?* | *When we look back on this decision one year from now, how will we know we did the right/best thing?* |
| *What can you tell me that will help me understand the importance of this issue to you?* | *If your teenager asked why you made this decision, what would you say to her?* |
| *What is significant about this question for you?* | *How would you explain the basis for the decision if the daily newspaper ran a front-page story on this issue, examining the decision you propose to make?* |
| *What is at risk in this issue?* | |
| *What worries you about this issue?* | |
| **Considering Stakeholders** | **Ethics and Principles** |
| *What do you think our duties and obligations are in this situation?* | *How do we know that this is the right thing to do?* |
| *Who should we be concerned about as we make this decision? Why?* | *How do we know this is not the right thing to do?* |
| *Who do you think will be affected by our decision?* | *What makes this an inappropriate way to proceed?* |
| *What seems to be important to them?* | *What standard(s) should we use to make a decision?* |
| *What standards do you think they (name a stakeholder group) will use to judge the fairness/rightness/goodness of our decision?* | *What criteria should we use to determine the best approach?* |
| *What do you think the effects/consequences (intended and unintended) of our decision will be for others?* | *Why do you think this is a good decision?* |
| *What criteria will our stakeholders use to evaluate our decision?* | *Why don't you think this is a good decision?* |
| | *What would you do if it were your decision? Why?* |
| | *If ——————— (a person you respect for her wisdom and integrity) were here and we asked for her perspective, what would she say to us?* |

## Worksheet for Step 2: Comprehend What Matters

**Introduction**

Talking with and listening to others enriches the decision-maker's understanding of what's at stake. Always adapt what you do to the context and the time available. The simple act of expressing to someone else what is important and hearing them reflect back what they understood offers a valuable opportunity to learn how one sees the issue and its essential aspects. The range of "what matters" includes organizational values, professional values, personal values, and values of others.

**Activity**

Enter into dialogue with others to develop a comprehensive list of important values. Be persistent in clarifying what others mean when they name a value. Use ordinary language and speak to what the value means in context.

**Steps to Take**

☞ By yourself, write down a list of all the things that matter in this situation. Go beyond your own point of view and consider what matters to others (stakeholders), directly or indirectly. Pay particular attention to those who stand to gain or lose.

✠ As a group, take turns and give each person the opportunity to briefly state a value he has identified. Go beyond big words such as "quality" or "integrity" and explain concretely what this value means to you in this context. Continue to take turns until you have exhausted what people have to say or you have run out of time. To slow down the exchange and work for greater clarity, consider asking someone to summarize the previous speaker by reflecting back what she understood him to mean. If the speaker needs to clarify, do so before the next person takes a turn.

✠ If time permits, develop a list on a pad, flip chart, or white board that captures the range of values identified. Test the comprehensiveness of the list by asking a few questions:

- *"What don't we understand about what is important?"*
- *"Whom aren't we thinking about?"*
- *"What are we missing?"*

## Pair Analysis

---

Compare each important value against others, one at a time, to determine which is more important. Place the letter of the more important value in the blank space with a number 1 = somewhat more important; 2 = clearly more important; 3 = much more important
   Add numbers from both sides of grid to get overall total for values

|  | Value A | Value B | Value C | Value D |  | Total |
|---|---|---|---|---|---|---|
| Value A | X | Example: B2 |  |  |  |  |
| Value B | X | X |  |  |  |  |
| Value C | X | X | X |  |  |  |
| Value D | X | X | X | X |  |  |
|  |  |  |  |  |  |  |
| Total |  |  |  |  |  |  |

## Worksheet for Step 3: Commit to What Matters Most

| | |
|---|---|
| **Introduction** | Every decision is based upon one or more things that matter. Intentional, reflective decision-makers must be clear about which values are most important to them. We call these most-weighty values the "guiding stars." They point the way toward action. |
| **Activity** | Offer all participants the opportunity to speak directly to "the heart of the matter." As important as what each person believes to be most important are the reasons that get them to that conclusion. To encourage forthright speech, it is essential to listen respectfully whether you agree or not. |
| **Steps to Take** | ☞ Make sure that everyone understands whose decision this is. |

✐ By yourself, review the list of values developed by the group (or from the previous worksheet). Write down three that you judge to be most important that should drive the choice among available options. Also write down your reasons for your selections.

✐ As a group, conduct an advocacy round. Take turns. Each person names one important value and briefly states the reason it is key. If someone is unclear about the speaker's value or the reason for its selection, follow up to clarify. Continue to go around, until everyone has had the opportunity to advocate for the top values.

✐ As a group, let the decision-maker summarize what he has heard. Help him consider key themes:

- *"Where do we seem to be in agreement?"*
- *"Where is there broad support, if not consensus?"*
- *"Where is there disagreement or conflict among participants?"*

✐ As a group, write down the short list of key values articulated by the decision-maker that will guide the selection among options in the next step.

## Decision Matrix

| Criteria | Relative Weight | Rate each as to how well it satisfies each value, 3 = high, 1 = low  Weight × rating = Score | | | |
| --- | --- | --- | --- | --- | --- |
| | | Option 1 | Option 2 | Option 3 | Option 4 |
| Example: Job security for our employees | 25% | 3 Score .75 | | | |
| Value A. _____ | | | | | |
| Value B. _____ | | | | | |
| Value C. _____ | | | | | |
| Value D. _____ | | | | | |
| Value E. _____ | | | | | |
| | | | | | |
| | | | | | |
| | | | | | |
| Total Score | 100% | | | | |

## Balance Sheet

**Option Under Consideration**

| To Honor This Value,<br>Do Not Choose this Option | _____ | To Honor This Value,<br>Choose this Option |
|---|---|---|

*Select key values to use as decision criteria.*

↓

Value A.
_____

Value B.
_____

Value C.
_____

Value D.
_____

Value E.
_____

**Consider the Risks**

| | |
|---|---|
| Introduction | The term "risk management" has become common in organizational life. All difficult choices also involve risk in some form. In addition to economic or legal risks, there are other risks that deserve consideration. Is there a risk to our credibility, a risk to the morale of the workforce, a risk to the relationship, a risk to mental or physical health? When a risk gets our attention, it is because something that matters to us, something we *value*, is in jeopardy. The greater the potential impact and the greater the likelihood of occurrence, the more thoroughly we should assess the risks *before* deciding. |
| Activity | Look more deeply at the potential consequences that may follow your decision. Consider two questions. First, what is the magnitude of the impact in terms of number of people and degree of harm or burden? Second, how likely is the consequence to occur? |

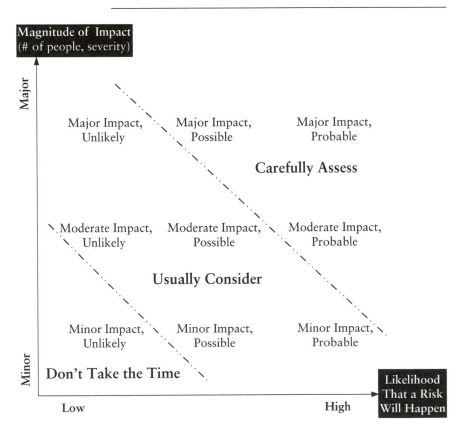

**Worksheet for Step 4: Choose to Act**

**Introduction**

Every decision is based upon something that matters. For a decision-maker who wants her choice to have integrity, the essential task is to make a choice that is genuinely connected to the guiding values. This connection provides a credible foundation for communicating to others.

**Activity**

Find the best fit between available options and the guiding values by testing each option against them. Before settling upon the best course of action, take a close look at the downside of your choice.

**Steps to Take**

✐ As a group, consider the options already identified. If there is time to search for additional options, do so and add them to the list. It may be useful to list the options on a flip chart or white board.

✐ As a group, listen to the decision-maker express the values he believes should guide the decision. If the decision-maker wants feedback from others present, this is the time for comments.

✐ As a group, look carefully at the option the decision-maker has chosen. Answer the following questions:

- *"What negative or undesirable consequences are likely or possible as a result of this decision?"*
- *"What do we regret about this decision?"*
- *"Are there important values that this decision does not honor?"*

**Mitigating Downside Impacts**

| | |
|---|---|
| Introduction | Most attempts decision-makers undertake to reduce or eliminate the recognized negative impacts of a decision don't help. When the effort is half-hearted or insincere, the decision-maker's credibility is at risk. |
| Activity | Identify and commit to concrete action to address the impact of your decision on others. |
| Steps to Take | ✐ Be specific. Under-promise and over-deliver! |

*"What will be done?"*

*"Who will do it?"*

*"When will it happen?"*

*"How will you communicate with others about the follow-up?"*

*"What is your commitment about this action?"*

☞ Make sure you do not:

- make general statements of intention
- communicate empathy that rings hollow without action and commitment
- attempt to minimize the burden that others may experience
- offer ideas that have been poorly thought through.

**Worksheet for Step 5: Communicate Transparently**

| | |
|---|---|
| **Introduction** | Many decisions fail to attract necessary support because they are communicated poorly to stakeholders. Effective communication requires honesty. |
| **Activity** | Prepare to communicate openly with those who should hear about the decision. |
| **Steps to Take** | ✒ State the decision in direct, simple language. Be clear who owns the decision. |

*"Every member of the board voted in favor of changing the terms of the benefits plan."*

✒ Consider whether it will help to tell the story of how you reached your conclusion (steps you took, who was involved, whom you consulted, the level of time and effort involved). *"Let me give you a sense of the road we took to reach our decision."*

✒ Identify the values that guided the decision. Use concrete, everyday language. *"We believe our commitment to our employees must remain our top priority. To keep this commitment, our benefit plan has to be as good as or better than anything our competition offers."*

☞ Make sure you are candid about the downside of this decision.

- **Negative Impacts:** *"I recognize that a likely result of this decision will be. . . However, in my judgment, this does not outweigh the importance of. . .because. . ."*
- **Values Not Honored:** *"Loyalty to our employees is important to us. We could not give it the highest priority at this time because. . . "*

## Moving through the Steps

### 1. Clarify Perspective

| Transition Language to Move On | Indicators of Readiness to Move On | Indicators of Need to Slow Down/Back Up |
|---|---|---|
| *Now that we understand some of the points of view we bring to this decision, let's take some time to identify what seems important to each of us.* | – Participants already beginning to name values.<br>– Impatience by key members of group (you can always come back to framing). | – Heated statements that indicate strong judgment about others' points of view.<br>– Inability to listen and understand what others are saying. |

### 2. Comprehend What Matters

| Transition Language to Move On | Indicators of Readiness to Move On | Indicators of Need to Slow Down/Back Up |
|---|---|---|
| *We have a list of what's important. Now let's take a look at the list and get a sense of whether any of these values are most important.* | – A list of important values on the flip chart.<br>– Affirmative response by group members to the question, "Are these clear as stated?" | – Inability to speak to the concerns of important stakeholders.<br>– Inability to listen and understand what others are saying.<br>– Missing essential information. |

### 3. Commit to What Matters Most

| Transition Language to Move On | Indicators of Readiness to Move On | Indicators of Need to Slow Down/Back Up |
|---|---|---|
| *Let's take this shorter list of key values and begin to look at the options we have in light of what we know must drive our decision.* | – A shorter, weighted list of the most important values from the larger list of all important values on the flip chart.<br>– Each person has been offered the opportunity to express (through advocacy, voting, or other method) her sense of relative importance. | – Inability to speak to the concerns of important stakeholders.<br>– Inability to listen and understand what others are saying.<br>– Comments by participants that indicate a lack of clear understanding of the values list.<br>– Missing essential information. |

### 4. Choose to Act

| Transition Language to Move On | Indicators of Readiness to Move On | Indicators of Need to Slow Down/Back Up |
|---|---|---|
| *We have a decision, so let's clarify how we will report this decision to those who need to hear about it.* | – A clear choice about how to proceed based on the options available and the key values.<br>– Affirmative response by group members to the question, "Is this what we agree to do?" | – Lack of knowledge about the range of options that are available.<br>– Inability to speak to the concerns of important stakeholders and impacts upon them from particular options.<br>– Inability to listen and understand what others are saying.<br>– Missing essential information. |

## 5. Communicate Transparently

| Transition Language to Move On | Indicators of Readiness to Move On | Indicators of Need to Slow Down/Back Up |
|---|---|---|
| None | – A completed decision summary form.<br>– Agreement on how the report will be made (by whom, when, where). | – If consensus is necessary or desirable, lack of support for the decision summary content.<br>– Lack of knowledge about stakeholder impacts. |

## Using the "On-the-Fly" Process

| *Ask the Right Question* | *Get Good Answers* |
|---|---|
| Step 1. *What point of view do I bring to this decision?* | ? Make sure everyone gets involved and responds briefly to the basic question.<br>? If there is time, follow up with another round and ask *What assumptions, if any, are you making about this decision?* THEN, keep these different perspectives in mind when people identify and discuss what matters so the dialogue can deepen. |
| Step 2. *What is important to the organization, to me, and to others?* | ? With the time available, hear briefly from everyone to build as comprehensive a list as possible of what is important to all stakeholders. Break down the big words... "Stewardship," "Integrity," and "Quality" by saying what they mean in this situation.<br>? Take time to reflect back what you are understanding to confirm key points and insure clarity. |
| Step 3. *What are the most important values that should guide our decision?* | ? Ask each person to advocate for the most important values that should guide the decision.<br>? Make sure that everyone clarifies the reason(s) for the choice of top values. These reasons are important to understand so everyone has a chance to influence others and be heard. |
| Step 4. *Which option is the best fit with the guiding values?* | ? Consider all the available options and determine which aligns most closely with the guiding values.<br>? Make sure you consider the down side of your choice BEFORE a final decision.<br>? Who will it hurt? Which important values don't receive priority? |
| Step 5. *How can we credibly communicate this decision to others who deserve to know?* | ? Use a decision worksheet form to cover the key communication elements.<br>? Don't shortchange the down side. Others will see it. If you don't acknowledge the problems with the decision and make it clear these issues were considered, the decision may lack support and your credibility could suffer. |

---

YES, BUT we only have 15 minutes! Speak directly and clearly about organizational core values by answering two questions. *1. How do our core values apply here? AND...2. What should we do to honor them to the greatest degree possible?*
YES, BUT we only have 30 minutes! Take shortcuts. Collapse Steps 1–3 into one step by using a compound question: *What is most important here that should guide our decision?* OR... Make each step a "lightning round" by asking everyone to respond very briefly. Limit or eliminate any discussion, comment, or follow up. At least, the decision-maker gets the benefit of multiple perspectives in summary form.

## When to Use a Values Process: A Decision Tree for Leaders

| | |
|---|---|
| Introduction | Leaders set the tone in organizations. The way they handle important issues sends a message to others about how business is to be conducted. It is critical that leaders identify important decision opportunities to bring the organization's values alive. |
| Activity | Identify decisions that require a deliberate values-based approach. |

---

**1. Initiator brings need for a decision to the leader or leader determines a decision is needed.**

**2. Leader assesses problem and determines if any of these criteria apply to the decision.**

**A. IMPORTANCE** – Will it influence the handling of future issues?
e.g. formal policy, "forks in the road," informal precedent ——— NO ——— **Make decision in preferred way**

**B. IMPACT** – Will it have significant consequences for affected stakeholders?
e.g. beginning or ending services, strategic choices, perceived "take-aways"

**C. RESOURCES** – Does it involve the allocation of a significant amount of limited resources?
e.g. major budget items, personnel changes, programmatic shifts

**D. PROFILE** – Is it likely to have high visibility?
e.g. media coverage, employee "buzz," concerns of partners, clients and others

**E. CREDIBILITY** – Is it important to establish or build trust and credibility with affected stakeholders at this time?
e.g. low morale, cynicism, need for buy-in

YES

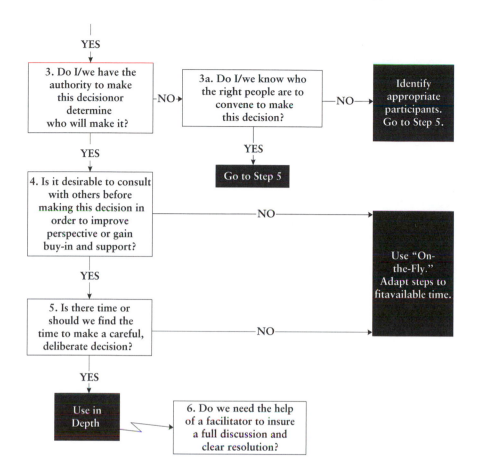

## Using the Steps in Your Organization

---

| When to Use This Approach | Groundwork |
|---|---|
| • **Importance:** Could the decision influence the handling of future issues?<br>• **Impact:** Could the decision have a significant impact on stakeholders?<br>• **Resources:** Does the decision involve the allocation of a significant amount of human, economic, or other resources?<br>• **Profile:** Will the decision have high visibility, internally or externally? | • Do we have enough information to proceed?<br>• Who should participate in this process and who will lead?<br>• How will the decision be made and who will make it? (Consensus, majority vote, individual)<br>• What is the role of this group? (Decision-maker, recommendation, consultation only)<br>• How much time do we require? |

**Step 1: CLARIFY...*What point of view do I bring to this decision?***
*Outcome:* Awareness and clarity about differing perspectives

• Make sure everyone gets involved and responds briefly to the basic question. If there is time, follow up with another round and ask, "What assumptions, if any, are we making about this situation and our decision?" Then, keep these different perspectives in mind when people discuss what matters to them so the dialogue can deepen.

**Step 2: COMPREHEND...*What is important to the organization, to me, and to those affected by this decision?***
*Outcome:* List of values to consider

• Take time to hear briefly from everyone and build a comprehensive list of what is important to stakeholders. Define big values words (Integrity, Quality, Fairness) by saying what they mean to you in this situation. Take time to reflect back what you hear to insure clarity of understanding and confirm key points.

**Step 3: COMMIT...*What are the most important values that should guide the decision?***
*Outcome:* A short list of key values

• Ask each person to advocate for the most important values that should guide the decision. Make sure everyone gives the reasoning for the values they advocate. Allow time to discuss the key values so everyone has a chance to influence others and be heard.

**Step 4: CHOOSE...*Which option is the best fit with the guiding values?***
*Outcome:* Coherent alignment between values and action

• Develop a set of options to consider and determine which one aligns most closely with the guiding values. Make sure you consider the downside of your choice BEFORE finalizing the decision.—Who will be affected?—Which important values do not receive priority?

**Step 5: COMMUNICATE...*How will we communicate this decision?***
*Outcome:* A credible decision that merits support

• Use the decision worksheet to prepare a clear, honest account of the decision. Address the downside and acknowledge any issues you struggled with in making the decision.

## Organizational Values Survey

| | |
|---|---|
| Introduction | Leaders set the tone in organizations. The way they handle important issues sends a message to others about how business is to be conducted. Leaders must understand how their actions and omissions are viewed by others in order to build a healthy climate within the organization. |
| Activity | Survey employees formally or interview them informally using some or all of the following questions to assess the reputation and credibility of leaders and managers in the area of decision-making and integrity. |

*1. Leaders and managers communicate important decisions in the organization to employees directly and openly so they understand the reasons for the decision.*

← -------------------------------------------------------------------- →

| 1 | 2 | 3 | 4 | 5 |
|---|---|---|---|---|
| Strongly Disagree | Disagree | | Agree | Strongly Agree |

*2. When leaders and managers communicate important decisions to employees, they acknowledge the negative impacts of the decision along with its benefits.*

← -------------------------------------------------------------------- →

| 1 | 2 | 3 | 4 | 5 |
|---|---|---|---|---|
| Strongly Disagree | Disagree | | Agree | Strongly Agree |

*3. The mission and core values of our organization are clear.*

← -------------------------------------------------------------------- →

| 1 | 2 | 3 | 4 | 5 |
|---|---|---|---|---|
| Strongly Disagree | Disagree | | Agree | Strongly Agree |

*4. I believe the stated core values of the organization are used to make important decisions.*

← -------------------------------------------------------------------- →

| 1 | 2 | 3 | 4 | 5 |
|---|---|---|---|---|
| Strongly Disagree | Disagree | | Agree | Strongly Agree |

*5. Leaders and managers in this organization do a good job consulting employees to understand different perspectives before making important decisions.*

← -------------------------------------------------------------------- →

| 1 | 2 | 3 | 4 | 5 |
|---|---|---|---|---|
| Strongly Disagree | Disagree | | Agree | Strongly Agree |

*6. Overall, the level of credibility of leaders and managers in this organization is high.*

← -------------------------------------------------------------------- →

| 1 | 2 | 3 | 4 | 5 |
|---|---|---|---|---|
| Strongly Disagree | Disagree | | Agree | Strongly Agree |

*Please add additional comments about how important decisions are made and communicated in the organization.*

## Map Stakeholder Values

**Introduction**    Individuals and groups who take an interest in a decision can be thought of as stakeholders. The sustainability of the decision and the credibility of the decision-maker(s) can be affected by the response of stakeholders to the decision. Therefore, it is prudent to consider their concerns.

**Activity**    When appropriate, consult directly to find out what matters to others. When this is not possible, make an educated guess as to what they would say if asked.

Diagram

> Those who must implement this decision hold the following values:

> Makers of this decision hold the following values:

> Others who may review this decision hold the following values:

> The decision under consideration is:

> Those who will formally review of this decision hold the following values:

> Beneficiaries of this decision hold the following values:

> Those who may experience negative consequences from this decision hold the following values:

# References and Sources for Quotations

## Introduction

Eleanor Roosevelt. *Think Exist.com Quotations Online*, http://en.thinkexist.com/quotes/eleanor_roosevelt/ (accessed September 13, 2005).

Alfred Korzybski. "American Mathematical Society paper" (1931), cited in *Wikipedia: The Free Encyclopedia*, http://en.wikipedia.org/wiki/The_map_is_not_the_territory.

Madame Curie. *The Quotations Page*, http://www.quotationspage.com (accessed September 13, 2005).

Issac Newton. *Think Exist.com Quotations Online*, http://en.thinkexist.com/quotes/issac_newton/ (accessed September 13, 2005).

Robert Frost. *The Poetry of Robert Frost*, ed. Edward Connery Lathem (New York: Holt, Rinehart, Winston, 1969), 105.

## Chapter 1

Talmud. Listed at http://www.care-givers.com/pages/inspiration/morequotes.

Peter Drucker. "Management: Tasks, Responsibilities, Practices," in *Quotationary*, ed. Leonard Roy Frank (New York: Random House, 2001), 591.

Edward R. Murrow television broadcast, December 31, 1955, *The Quotations Page*, http://www.quotationspage.com (accessed September 13, 2005).

Abraham Maslow. *The Quotations Page*, http://www.quotationspage.com (accessed September 13, 2005).

Ludwig Wittgenstein. "Culture and Value, 1977," trans. Peter Winch, 1980, in *Quotationary*, ed. Leonard Roy Frank (New York: Random House, 2001), 761.

John Dewey. Listed in www.hpstrategy.com/html/quotes.html.

Popular bumper sticker. www.cafepress.com

Popular saying. Listed in *Quotationary*, ed. Leonard Roy Frank (New York: Random House, 2001), 345.

Thomas Merton. "No Man Is an Island," in *Quotationary*, ed. Leonard Roy Frank (New York: Random House, 2001), 703.

Peter Drucker. "The Effective Executive," in *Quotationary*, ed. Leonard Roy Frank (New York: Random House, 2001), 263.

## Chapter 2

Martin Luther King Jr. Quoted in Jocelyn Elders, "Someone Had to Speak Up," *New York Times*, December 20, 1994, in *Quotationary*, ed. Leonard Roy Frank (New York: Random House, 2001), 788.

Senegalese Proverb. Listed in http://www.walkthetalk.com /lookinside/managers_communication_handbook.01.pdf.

George Lakoff and Mark Johnson, *Metaphors We Live By* (Chicago: University of Chicago Press, 1980), 231–32.

Alfred North Whitehead. Listed in *Quotationary*, ed. Leonard Roy Frank (New York: Random House, 2001), 695.

Roy Disney. *Brainy Quote*, http://www.brainyquote.com/quotes/quotes/d/ (accessed on September 13, 2005).

Epictetus. *Think Exist.com Quotations Online*, http://en.thinkexist.com/quotes/epictetus/ (accessed September 13, 2005).

St. Frances de Sales. *The Quotations Page*, http://www.quotationspage.com (accessed September 13, 2005).

Malvina Reynolds. "Dialogue, cited at *Co-Intelligence Institute*, http://www.co-intelligence.org/P-dialogue.html.

Oliver Wendell Holmes Jr. *Think Exist.com Quotations Online*, http://en.thinkexist.com/quotes/oliver_wendell_holmes/ (accessed September 13, 2005).

## Chapter 3

Carl Schurz. *Think Exist.com Quotations Online*, http://en.thinkexist.com/quotes/carl_schurz/ (accessed September 13, 2005).

Stephen Covey. *First Things First* (New York: Fireside, 1994), cited at http://app.outreach.psu.edu/weidemann/InsideOutreach121503.pdf.

Bill Cosby. *Think Exist.com Quotations Online*, http://en.thinkexist.com/quotes/bill_cosby/ (accessed September 13, 2005).

Justice William O. Douglas. *Think Exist.com Quotations Online*, http://en.thinkexist.com/quotes/bill_cosby/ (accessed September 13, 2005).

Georgia O'Keefe. Cited at *Antiques and the Arts Online*, http://www.antiquesandthearts.com/CS-2005-02-15-13-28-15p2.htm.

Benjamin Tregoe. Cited in George Dixon, *What Works At Work: Lessons From the Masters* (Minneapolis: Lakewood, 1988), 256.

Albert Einstein. *Quoteland*, http://www.quoteland.com/author.asp?AUTHOR_ID=89 (accessed September 13, 2005).

William James. Listed in *Quotationary*, ed. Leonard Roy Frank (New York: Random House, 2001), 864.

Bertrand Russell. "Knowledge and Wisdom," in *Portraits From Memory, and Other Essays*, 1956. Listed in *Quotationary*, ed. Leonard Roy Frank (New York: Random House, 2001), 930.

Heraclitus. *Columbia World of Quotations*, http://www.bartleby.com.

## Chapter 4

Edmund Burke. *Think Exist.com Quotations Online*, http://en.thinkexist.com/quotes/edmund_burke/ (accessed September 13, 2005).

Franz Grillmarzer. Primalaus, in *Libusssa*, Act 3 (1872), listed in http://www.poemhunter.com/quotations (accessed September 13, 2005).

William James. *Think Exist.com Quotations Online*, http://en.thinkexist.com/quotes/william_james/ (accessed September 13, 2005).

David Crockett. *Think Exist.com Quotations Online*, http://en.thinkexist.com/quotes/david_crockett/ (accessed September 13, 2005).

Gautama Buddha. Cited at http://www.gatheringin.com/love.html.

La Rochefoucauld. *Maxims*, 89 (1665), trans. Leonard Tancock (1959), listed in *Quotationary*, ed. Leonard Roy Frank (New York: Random House, 2001), 502.

Jean Paul Sartre. *Notebook on Ethics*, trans. David Pellauer (Chicago: University of Chicago, 1992).

Thomas Jefferson. *The Quotations Page*, http://www.quotationspage.com (accessed September 13, 2005).

Aristotle. http://www.en.wikiquote.org/wiki/Aristotle.

Norman Cousins. "Editor's Odyssey: Gleanings from Articles and Editorials by N.C.," ed. Susan Schieflebein, *Saturday Review*, 15 April 1978.

Martin Luther King, Jr. *Brainy Quote* http://www.brainyquote.com (accessed on September 13, 2005).

Mason Cooley. *City Aphorisms, Ninth Selection* (New York: 1992), listed in http://www.poemhunter.com (accessed September 13, 2005).

Plato. *Laches, or Courage*, http://classics.mit.edu/Plato/laches/html.

Robert Frost. "The Road Not Taken," *The Poetry of Robert Frost* (Holt, Rinehart, and Winston: New York, 1969), 105.

G.K. Chesterton. *Think Exist.com Quotations Online*, http://en.thinkexist.com/quotes/g._k._chesterton/ (accessed September 13, 2005).

## Chapter 5

Seneca the Younger. "On Practicing What You Preach," in *Moral Letters to Lucilius*, 14.2, trans. Richard Gummere (1918), in *Quotationary*, ed. Leonard Roy Frank (New York: Random House, 2001), 930.

Charles Frankel. *The Case for Modern Man* (New York: Harper 1955), cited at http://www.mnforsustain.org.

Edward R. Murrow. *Think Exist.com Quotations Online*, http://en.thinkexist.com/quotes/edward_r_murrow/ (accessed September 13, 2005).

Robert E. Lee. *Robert E. Lee Quotes*, http://www.sonofthesouth.net/leefoundation/Notable%20Lee%20Quotes.htm.

Miguel Unamuno. Listed at http://www.nupge.ca/news_2004/n15no04a.htm.

Daniel Ellsberg. *Secrets: A Memoir of Vietnam and the Pentagon Papers* (New York: Viking, 2002), cited in "Secrets and Lies," http://www.commondreams.org/views02/1031-01.htm.

Karl Kraus. *Think Exist.com Quotations Online*, http://en.thinkexist.com/quotes/karl_kraus/ (accessed September 13, 2005).

Mark Twain. Cited at http://www.faculty.rsu.edu/~felwell/HomePage/aphorisms.htm.

William Blake. *Brainy Quote*, http://www.brainyquote.com/quotes/quotes/w/williambla150110.html (accessed September 13, 2005).

Ralph Waldo Emerson. *Think Exist.com Quotations Online*, http://en.thinkexist.com/quotes/ralph_waldo_emerson/ (accessed September 13, 2005).

Scott Adams. *Dilbert Gives You the Business* (Kansas City: McMeel Publishing, 1999), 175.

Dan Quayle. *Think Exist.com Quotations Online*, http://en.thinkexist.com/quotes/dan_quayle/ (accessed September 13, 2005).

## Chapter 6

Bernard Baruch. *Brainy Quote*, http://www.brainyquote.com/quotes/quotes/b/bernardbar181406.html (accessed on September 13, 2005).

Ralph Waldo Emerson. Journal, September 1848, listed in *Quotationary*, ed. Leonard Roy Frank (New York: Random House, 2001), 285.

Carl Jung. "Analytical Psychology and Education," *The Development of Personality*, trans. R.F.C. Hull, 1954, in *Quotationary*, ed. Leonard Roy Frank (New York: Random House, 2001), 387.

Yogi Berra. *The Yogi Book* (New York: Workman, 1998), 34.

Huang Po. Listed at *Belief Net*, http://www.beliefnet.com/story/135/story_13576_1.html.

Barbara J. McNeill, Stephen G. Pauker, Harold C. Sox, and Amos Tversky. "On the Elicitation Preferences for Alternative Therapies," *New England Journal of Medicine* 30621, 1982: 1259–62.

Demosthenes. *Olynthiaca, 3.19*, in *Quotationary*, ed. Leonard Roy Frank (New York: Random House, 2001), 763.

Thomas Powers. "The Sins of a President," *New York Times Book Review*, November 30, 1997.

Walter Lippmann. *Public Opinion*, 6.1, 1922.

Will Rogers. "Defending My Soup Plate Position," *The Illiterate Digest*, 1924.

A.E. Houseman. Lecture before the Faculties of Arts and Laws and of Science, University College, London, 3 October 1892, listed in *Quotationary*, ed. Leonard Roy Frank (New York: Random House, 2001), 196.

Roy Blitzer. Listed in *The Journal*, "Change, Liminality, and Transition Quotes" http://www.resonate.ca/journal/issues/2005/september/quote.htm (accessed September 13, 2005).

Aldous Huxley. "Beliefs," in *Ends and Means: An Inquiry into the Nature of Ideals and into the Methods Employed for Their Realization*, 1937 (reprint Westport, CT: Greenwood, 1969).

Benjamin Franklin. *Poor Richard's Almanack*, July, 1758 (reprint White Plains, NY: Peter Pauper Press, 1980).

## Chapter 7

James Tobin. *Ernie Pyle's War* (New York: The Free Press, 1997).

Audre Lorde. Quoted in *The CCASA Connection: Newsletter of the Colorado Coalition Against Sexual Assault*, December 1999.

Aurelio Sanchez. "Learning to Negotiate Cultural Identities," *Albuquerque Journal*, March 25, 2005.

Rita Charon. "Narrative Medicine: Form, Function, and Ethics," *Annals of Internal Medicine*, 2001: 134–84.

Raymond Cohen. *Negotiating across Cultures* (Washington, D.C.: U.S. Institute of Peace Press, 1999) 12.

John Fitzgerald Kennedy. *Columbia World of Quotations*, www.bartleby.com.

Hillary Rodham Clinton. *Columbia World of Quotations*, www.bartleby.com

Arthur Kleinman. *Patients and Healers in the Context of Culture* (Berkeley, CA: The Regents of the University of California, 1981).

Willa Cather. *Death Comes for the Archbishop*, 1927, Book VII, Ch. IV (reprint New York: Vintage Books, 1971).

Mohandas Gandhi. *Think Exist.com Quotations Online*, http://en.thinkexist.com/quotes/mahatma_gandhi/ (accessed September 13, 2005).

David Bohm. *Quoteland*, "Conformity & Nonconformity" http://www.quoteland.com/author.asp?AUTHOR_ID=1279 (accessed September 13, 2005).

## Chapter 8

John Kenneth Galbraith. *The Culture of Contentment* (New York: Houghton Mifflin,1992), 6.

American saying. Listed in *Quotationary*, ed. Leonard Roy Frank (New York: Random House, 2001), 868.

Ovid. Listed in *Quotationary*, ed. Leonard Roy Frank (New York: Random House, 2001), 868.

Terrence Deal and Allan Kennedy. *Corporate Cultures: The Rites and Rituals of Corporate Life*, listed in *Quotationary*, ed. Leonard Roy Frank (New York: Random House, 2001), 152.

Edward Luttwak. *Coup d'Etat: A Practical Handbook*, listed in *Quotationary*, ed. Leonard Roy Frank (New York: Random House, 2001), 572.

Mary McCarthy. *Think Exist.com Quotations Online*, http://en.thinkexist.com/quotes/mary_mccarthy/ (accessed September 13, 2005).

Irving Janis. *Groupthink*, 2nd ed. (New York: Houghton Mifflin, 1986).

Miguel de Unamuno. Cited at http://www.healthyplace.com/communities/depression/related/self_help_2.asp.

Robert G. Ingersoll. "Fragments," *The Philosophy of Ingersoll*, ed. Vere Goldthwaite, (1906), in *Quotationary*, ed. Leonard Roy Frank (New York: Random House, 2001), 94.

Warren Bennis. Preface (closing words) to *Leaders on Leadership: Interviews with Top Executives*, in *Quotationary*, ed. Leonard Roy Frank (New York: Random House, 2001), 440.

James MacGregor Burns. *Leadership*, in *Quotationary*, ed. Leonard Roy Frank, (New York: Random House, 2001), 441.

Martin Luther King, Jr. *Where Do We Go From Here: Chaos or Community?*, in *Quotationary*, ed. Leonard Roy Frank (New York: Random House, 2001), 444.

Herbert Spencer. *Social Statics*, in *Quotationary*, ed. Leonard Roy Frank (New York: Random House, 2001), 883.

Talleyrand. *Think Exist.com Quotations Online*, http://en.thinkexist.com/quotes/Charles_M._de_Talleyrand/ (accessed September 13, 2005).

Chinese proverb. *Think Exist.com Quotations Online*, http://en.thinkexist.com/quotes/chinese_proverbs/ (accessed September 13, 2005).

## Chapter 9

Barry Lopez. *Arctic Dreams* (Vintage: 2001), listed in *Think Exist.com Quotations Online*, http://en.thinkexist.com/quotes/barry_lopez/ (accessed September 13, 2005).

# Annotated Bibliography

Badaracco, Joseph L., Jr. *Defining Moments: When Managers Must Choose between Right and Right*. Boston: Harvard Business School Press, 1997. An engaging analysis of right vs. right decisions in the work place, and the role of personal values in resolving such dilemmas. The author emphasizes philosophical content and questions as the means to address the challenge of difficult decisions. The book covers work and life choices using illustrations of manager dilemmas referred to as "defining moments" because they define the decision-maker's identity and fundamental values.

Cohen, Randy. *The Good, the Bad, and the Difference: How to Tell Right from Wrong in Everyday Situations*. New York: Random House, 2003. An entertaining, well-written, and witty series of essays, many of them based on material from Cohen's weekly column, "The Ethicist," published in the *New York Times Magazine*. While focused primarily on "right vs. wrong" issues, Cohen helps the reader dig down to the values level of a dilemma.

Cohen, Raymond. *Negotiating across Cultures: International Communication in an Interdependent World*. 2nd rev. ed. Washington, D.C.: United States Institute of Peace, 1999. An analysis of how cultural differences affect international negotiations. In the Prelude to the book, Cohen observes: "One of the characteristics of any vibrant society is its ability to assimilate foreign influences while remaining true to its essential beliefs and motifs."

Gardner, Howard. *Changing Minds: The Art and Science of Changing Our Own and Other People's Minds*. Boston: Harvard Business School, 2004. The author, a noted psychologist and educational theorist, maps the territory of mind change. He identifies seven levers that help or hinder and illustrates his ideas with a wide range of examples of famous and ordinary people.

Goleman, Daniel. *Vital Lies, Simple Truths: The Psychology of Self Deception*. New York: Simon and Schuster, 1985. An accessible psychology text on how the mind works, especially the nature of consciousness—what we pay attention to, what we ignore or avoid, and why. Goleman analyzes and identifies some of the common traps we fall into as we construct our social reality.

Goleman, Daniel, Richard Boyatzis, and Annie McKee. *Primal Leadership: Realizing the Power of Emotional Intelligence*. Boston: Harvard Business School, 2002. In this groundbreaking book on the emotional dimension of leadership, the authors focus on leaders' awareness of their values and the role this awareness plays in making and communicating decisions to others.

Hall, E.T. *Beyond Culture*. New York: Doubleday Anchor, 1976. A classic on culture and Western society's failure to understand both itself and others. Drawing from his background in psychoanalysis and anthropology, Hall observes in Chapter 1: "[I]n his strivings for order, Western man has created chaos by denying that part of his self that integrates while enshrining the parts that fragment experience."

Hammond, John S., Ralph L. Keeney, and Howard Raiffa. *Smart Decisions: A Practical Guide to Making Better Life Decisions*. Boston: Harvard Business School Press, 1999. The authors lay out a cognitive approach for the individual decision-maker. They sum up the steps with the acronym, "PrOACT," for problem, objectives, alternatives, consequences, tradeoffs. The audience is the individual decision-maker, and the decisions described cover a broad spectrum of daily choices people must make.

Issacs, William. *Dialogue and the Art of Thinking Together*. New York: Currency/Doubleday, 1999. The author is the founder of the "Dialogue Project" at MIT. He makes an elegant plea for thinking together by including listening in our use of language, both in the business world and in our personal lives. The book draws on the author's experience with major corporations and demystifies the practice of dialogue.

Janis, Irving L. *Groupthink*. 2nd ed. New York: Houghton Mifflin, 1986. Janis, in this now famous work, explains the dynamics that silence dissent and forge false consensus. He provides a series of historic case studies to illustrate key points.

Kahneman, Daniel and Amos Tversky, eds. *Choices, Values, and Frames*. Cambridge: Cambridge University Press, 2000. The editors have been in the vanguard of the "decision sciences" for decades. Here they have collected an anthology of fairly technical articles on the cognitive and psychophysical determinants of decision-making, in both risky and riskless contexts. Various authors explain common traps such as risk aversion and risk seeking behavior in different situations.

Kaner, Sam, Lenny Lind, Catherine Toldi, Sarah Fisk, and Duane Berger. *Facilitator's Guide to Participatory Decision-making*. Gabriola Island, British Columbia: New Society Publishers, 1996. A practical guide for working with groups engaged in collaborative decision-making. The book offers guidance for facilitators, an analysis of group dynamics, and techniques for creating sustainable agreements.

Kidder, Rushworth M. *How Good People Make Tough Choices: Resolving the Dilemmas of Ethical Living*. New York: William Morrow, 1995. The first comprehensive look at right vs. right choices we face in everyday decision-making. Again, the audience is the individual decision-maker, and in his "Overview" to the book, Kidder addresses the reader: "This is a book for those who want to address and resolve tough choices through energetic self-reflection."

Klein, Gary. *Sources of Power: How People Make Decisions*. Cambridge: MIT Press, 1998. The author spent a decade carefully observing how experienced fire commanders, fighter pilots, paramedics, and others make difficult decisions. From these observations, he lays out a "naturalistic" approach to decision-making that identifies how decision-makers bring experience to bear, especially in crisis situations.

O'Toole, James. *Leading Change: The Argument for Values-Based Leadership*. San Francisco: Jossey-Bass, 1995. In a wide-ranging discourse covering art, business, philosophy and history, the author examines the nature of leadership that can effect change. He believes that leadership is about more than style. It is about ideas. Effective leadership requires that a leader create a "values-based umbrella" big enough to hold diverse constituencies while remaining focused and vital enough to mobilize and direct people's energies toward the pursuit of common goals.

Patterson, Kerry, Joseph Grenny, Ron McMillan, and Al Switzler. *Crucial Conversations: Tools for Talking When Stakes are High*. New York: McGraw-Hill, 2002. This book provides an analysis and prescription for effective conversations at home and at work when opinions vary, the stakes are high for at least one of the parties, and emotions are likely to spill over.

Russo, J. Edward and Paul J.H. Schoemaker. *Decision Traps: The Ten Barriers to Brilliant Decision-Making and How to Overcome Them*. New York: Simon and Schuster, 1989. The authors are academicians and corporate consultants who provide a coaching approach to common errors in decision-making and how to avoid them. Russo and Schoemaker draw on behavioral decision theory, an empirical field of study that describes how people actually do make decisions. The book provides readable digests of research studies that illustrate key points. The examples are largely taken from business settings.

Russo, J. Edward and Paul J.H Schoemaker. *Winning Decisions: Getting It Right the First Time*. New York: Doubleday, 2001. Like *Smart Decisions*, this book provides substantial content along with sound behavioral, workbook-like guidelines. The book targets a business audience and draws on numerous cases and issues from this setting.

Schwartz, Barry. *The Paradox of Choice: Why More Is Less*. New York: HarperCollins, 2004. A psychology professor describes how having too many choices can negatively impact our decisions. Too many choices can lead to decision-making paralysis and second-guessing one's choice, even before it's made. The book includes a summary of research, a mini-tutorial from the social sciences, and concrete steps to lower the stress level of decision-making.

Senge, Peter. *The Fifth Discipline Notebook: Building a Learning Organization.* New York: Doubleday, 1994. The lead author is the Founder and Director of the Center for Organizational Learning at MIT's Sloan School of Management. Senge and his collaborators offer lessons from their fieldwork on the leading edge of organizational systems and innovation. While they cover a wide range of topics related to effective organizational processes, they build on David Bohm's work, advocating dialogue and effective use of conversation in workplace decision-making.

Stone, Douglas, Bruce Patton, and Sheila Heen. *Difficult Conversations: How to Discuss What Matters Most.* New York: Viking, 1999. This book provides a diagram of the architecture of all difficult conversations. The authors describe the three components of such conversations: what happened, what feelings are involved, and what the conversation means to those involved.

Surowiecki, James. *The Wisdom of Crowds: Why the Many are Smarter Than the Few and How Collective Wisdom Shapes Businesses, Economies, Societies and Nations.* New York: Doubleday, 2004. At a time when we revere experts and elites, the book provides a compelling case in support of a fascinating hypothesis: people in groups are smarter than a few brilliant thinkers. Much of the book addresses systems of opinion such as stock markets and voting, but in one chapter on teams, committees, and juries, the author analyzes the dimensions of small group structure and process that contribute to good decisions.

Tannen, Deborah. *The Argument Culture: Moving from Debate to Dialogue.* New York: Random House, 1998. The author has produced a series of engaging offerings on the way conversation works and breaks down. In this book she tackles our tendency, especially in Western society, to treat public discourse as combat. "This book is about a pervasive warlike atmosphere that makes us approach public dialogue, and just about anything we need to accomplish, as if it were a fight."

von Oech, Roger. *A Kick in the Seat of the Pants.* New York: Harper and Row, 1986. A leading business consultant offers a rich menu of ideas and techniques for developing personal and group creativity.

Welch, David A. *Decisions, Decisions: The Art of Effective Decision-making.* New York: Prometheus Books, 2002. The author offers a nine step decision-making process, applicable to a wide range of decisions. Topics covered include gender, money and chance, judgment, and perception.

# Index

Note: Pages with illustrations are indicated by *italic* type.

# About the Authors

MARK D. BENNETT is the coauthor of *The Art of Mediation* (South Bend: NITA Press, 2nd. ed. 2005). He has been an adjunct professor at the University of New Mexico School of Law since 1987, teaching courses in general, family, and advanced mediation. His professional mediation experience over twenty-five years includes hundreds of cases: employment, civil rights, organizational, health care, divorce and family, land use, public policy, and commercial.

He graduated from the University of Texas School of Law, where he also received graduate and clinical training in counseling psychology and family therapy.

His current work focuses on the deliberate use of organizational, professional, and personal values in making difficult decisions. He offers leadership training and facilitates decision-making processes for a wide range of clients: federal agencies, state and local governments, community nonprofit groups, and corporations.

You may contact him at decisionres@cybermesa.com.

JOAN McIVER GIBSON is a philosopher and consultant in applied ethics, bioethics, and values-based decision-making. She has over thirty years of teaching, training, consulting, and administrative work in a variety of settings: universities, business, state and federal government, health care, community, and research organizations.

She graduated from Mount Holyoke College in 1965 and in 1974 earned her PhD in philosophy from the University of California at San Diego.

In 2003, she retired as the director of the University of New Mexico Health Sciences Ethics Program, and for twenty years she chaired a hospital ethics committee in Albuquerque, New Mexico. She is a coauthor of *Health Care Ethics Committees: The Next Generation* (Chicago: American Hospital Association, 1993). She has published numerous articles and book chapters on bioethics, applied ethics, ethics committees, and values-based decision-making.

Her current focus includes ethics and decision-making as well as a demonstration project to link children with their incarcerated parents through televideo technology.

You may contact her at miriam@unm.edu.